DIAGRAMMATICAL
ANALYSIS

DIAGRAMMATICAL ANALYSIS

Lee L. Kantenwein

Diagrammatical Analysis
Copyright ©1979 by Lee L. Kantenwein

ISBN 10: 0-88469-150-0
ISBN 13: 978-0-88469-150-1
RELIGION/Biblical Reference/Language Study

Translations of Bible texts are the author's.

Fourth Revised Edition
Eighth Printing, March 2007

Published by BMH Books
BMH Books, P.O. Box 544, Winona Lake, IN 46590 USA
www.bmhbooks.com

Printed in the United States of America

TABLE OF CONTENTS

PREFACE V

INTRODUCTION 1
   Diagrammatical Analysis Defined 1
   Diagrammatical Analysis Designed 3
   Diagrammatical Analysis Delineated 8
   Important Tips on Diagramming 10

CHAPTER I.   BASIC ILLUSTRATIVE DIAGRAM PATTERNS 13

SENTENCE ANALYSIS 13

   A. Simple Sentence 13

      1. Subject and Predicate
      2. Subject, Predicate, Direct Object and Objective Complement
      3. Subject, Predicate and Indirect Object
      4. Subject, Predicate and Subjective Complement, Predicate
         Nominative or Predicate Adjective
      5. Nouns in Apposition
      6. Adjectival and Adverbial Modifiers
      7. Prepositional Phrase

   B. Compound Subjects, Verbs, Objects and Modifiers 22

      1. Compound Subjects
      2. Compound Verbs
      3. Compound Objects
      4. Compound Modifiers

   C. Compound Sentence 26

   D. Complex Sentence 29

   E. Sentence Function 31

      1. Declarative Sentence
      2. Interrogative Sentence
      3. Imperative Sentence
      4. Exclamatory Sentence

PHRASE ANALYSIS 35

   A. Nominative Phrase 35

   B. Objective Phrase 36

   C. Prepositional Phrase 37

D. Participle Phrase 38
   1. As a Modifier
   2. As a Subject
   3. As a Verb
   4. As a Predicate Adjective or Direct Object

E. Infinitive Phrase 43
   1. As Subject of the Verb
   2. As Direct Object of the Verb
   3. As a Verb
   4. As a Modifier
   5. Usage in Indirect Discourse
   6. The Infinitive Absolute
   7. The Infinitive Construct

CLAUSE ANALYSIS 47

A. Relative Clause 47

B. Temporal Clause 50

C. Local Clause 50

D. Subordinating Clause 51

E. Purpose and Result Clauses 52

F. Comparative Clause 53

G. Concessive Clause 54

H. Conditional Clauses 55
   1. The Simple Condition
   2. The Contrary to Fact Condition
   3. The More Probable Future Condition
   4. The Less Probable Future Condition

I. Clause-al Connectives 61

SPECIALIZED ANALYSIS 63

A. Vocative 63

B. Conjunctions 64

C. Indirect Discourse 67

D. Nominative Absolute or Independent Nominative 68

E. Genitive Absolute 69

F. Double Accusative 70

G. Adverbial Accusative of Reference 71

H. Modifier(s) of Compound Units 72

I. Single Negative with Compound Verbs 72

J. The Particles μέν δέ 73

K. Complementary Infinitive 74

CHAPTER II. BASIC ILLUSTRATIVE SERMONIC
    ORGANIZATION 77

Simple Sentence with Modifiers on Single Base Line 79

Compound Subjects, Verbs, Objects and Modifiers on
    Single Base Line 80

Compound and Complex Sentences with Two or More
    Base Lines 81

Sentences with Phrases and Clauses 82

Sentences with the Vocative 82

Sentence Variations in Either Testament with a Simple
    Introductory Subject and Verb Such As: "Jesus said"
    or "The Lord of Hosts declared unto ..." 83

Sentences with Consistent Hebrew Parallelism on the
    Base Lines 84

Sentences with One Base Line and Many Modifiers under
    the Verb 84

Sentences Having a Compound Unit with One Modifier 86

Sentences in Either Testament Which Have an Abundance
    of Words Horizontally 86

Illustrated from Psalm 119:17–18 87
    Contextual Analysis
    Diagrammatical Analysis and Sermonic Structure
    Analytical Outline

Illustrated from 2 Peter 1:19–21 91
    Contextual Analysis
    Diagrammatical Analysis and Sermonic Structure
    Analytical Outline

Illustrated from Mark 6:20 100
    Contextual Analysis
    Analysis Word Sheets
    Diagrammatical Analysis and Sermonic Structure
    Analytical Outline
    Sermonic Outline

INDEX OF BIBLICAL REFERENCES 107

BIBLIOGRAPHY 109

PREFACE

Diagramming of English sentences was introduced to this author as a ninth grade student. The fascination of this methodological tool for learning grammar and syntactical relationships was intriguing. The technique became a discipline for learning not only English but also German and eventually Greek and Hebrew. It is this background that provides a basis for this manual.

Many inquiries have been made as to the origin of this manual. It began as a personal project in 1972 for a course "Greek Exegetical Methods." Students at Grace Theological Seminary heard about the venture and since there was no known beginning tool like it available, I was encouraged to put it in syllabus form for the benefit of the Grace Seminary students. However, the word got out and requests came from individuals and Christian educational institutions for copies which the seminary print shop was unable to fill. Therefore, a decision was made to publish the material which first appeared in 1979.

Originally, the syllabus was done only in Greek and Hebrew to illustrate basic recognized diagrammatical patterns. But because diagramming was new to a majority of students, the need existed to add an English basis for quicker comprehension of the methodology. Thus, English sentence analysis was included as the initial chapter with basic definitions regarding the parts of speech and grammatical terms used in diagramming. Chapter two contained the original work illustrating the methodology from the Greek and Hebrew with some examples added as questions arose concerning particular characteristics of the biblical text. Revisions and inclusions occurred as students and faculty made suggestions.

The major revision of the third edition brought the English, Greek and Hebrew analyses together in one chapter under each grammatical unit. Individual analyses peculiar to Greek and Hebrew primarily occurs at the end of chapter one.

The second chapter on sermonic organization is much the same as in the previous publications. A few revisions and additions are included for clarification.

Two ladies deserve special acknowledgment of gratitude: My wife, Phyllis, who not only has a rich ministry of music of her own, but who graciously tolerates my piles of books and papers and the many hours spent with the graphics of this work. Mrs. Joy Drake was my secretary who typed, cut, pasted, and helped arrange the material to put it in book form. Her cooperation, initiative, patience, and encouragement helped me to achieve the goal at hand.

A special note of appreciation is extended to Terry White and Jesse Deloe of BMH Books for their efforts in pursuing the goal of typesetting the Greek and Hebrew, and the new look for this manual. Gratitude is also extended to Valerie Levy of Drawing Board Studios who did the typesetting and typing to achieve the end product. It was not an easy task.

Lee L. Kantenwein
January 2007

INTRODUCTION

I believe in biblical inerrancy without apology. An energetic emphasis upon the Word of God is imperative. A workable knowledge of Greek and Hebrew is without equal. A truly effective Christian ministry involves the proclamation of the whole counsel (purpose) of God (Acts 20:27). A methodology which focuses upon the comprehension of the distinctive communication and the revelatory message of the inspired biblical writings is essential. Diagrammatical analysis of the biblical languages is an indispensable and methodological exegetical tool for the purpose of observing sentence structure and syntactical relationships.

Many sermonizers have never been instructed to diagram or have forgotten the method. Some have been trained that diagramming must always fit into select molds. Many individuals have never been taught the nomenclature of the parts of speech or their function. The problem is further compounded for many biblical interpreters because sermonic preparation should be based upon a syntactical analysis of the Hebrew and Greek texts. An exegetical expository preaching and teaching ministry of a "What saith the Scriptures?" is based upon a literal, contextual, historical, cultural, and grammatical interpretation. This five-fold basis must be maintained if diagrammatical analysis is to be used effectively.

DIAGRAMMATICAL ANALYSIS DEFINED

Analysis is the diagnosis of a sentence into its separate parts (words, phrases, clauses), and carefully scrutinizing each part in its relation to the whole. "When analysis is objectified in the form of a written diagram, it pictures relationships."[1] A diagram and/or diagramming is defined in various ways as follows:

> The diagram of a sentence is merely a way to study it by taking it apart. It is a picture that shows what each part of the sentence does and what its importance is.[2]

---

1. Owen L. Crouch, *Expository Preaching and Teaching—Hebrews* (Joplin, MO: College Press Publishing Company, 1983), p. xxxviii.
2. Donald H. Ludgin, "Diagram of a Sentence" in *The World Book Encyclopedia*, vol. 17, 1972, p. 240.

A Diagram is a pictorial portrayal of a sentence.[3]

Diagramming is a pictorial or graphic means of analyzing sentences; it enables one to see construction instead of trying to retain them in his head. It is a sort of grammatical shorthand whereby one is saved the necessity of writing phrases like 'the subject is' and 'the verb is' every time he is asked to analyze a sentence or a part of a sentence.[4]

A diagram is a picture of the offices and the relations of the different parts of a sentence.[5]

Diagramming is a brief graphic device for identifying and analyzing the grammatical relationships among the elements of a sentence.[6]

Diagramming is giving a picture of word relationships.[7]

An arrangement on lines to show relationships within the sentence.[8]

Analysis is that department of grammar which treats of the structure and nature of sentences, their separation into elements, and a description of these elements.[9]

These sample definitions reveal that diagrammatical analysis is "some kind of a graphic representation which can be of real assistance in systematizing and clarifying the structure of a sentence."[10] "When we resolve a sentence into its parts we are describing the function that every expression appearing in the given sentence performs."[11] Therefore, diagramming is a diagnosis of syntax serving to pinpoint the relation that

---

3. Louise M. Ebner, *Learning English with the Bible.* English Grammar Diagrams Based in the Book of Joshua, AMG Publishers, 1983. p. 7.

4. Kendall B. Taft, John Francis McDermott and Dana O. Jensen, *The Technique of Composition* (New York: Rinehart & Co., Inc., 1941), p. 12.

5. Alonzo Reed and Brainerd Kellogg, *Higher Lessons in English* (New York: Charles E. Merrill Co., 1909), p. 21.

6. Charles Vivian and Bernetta Jackson, *English Composition* (Barnes Noble, Inc., 1961), pp. 242–43.

7. J. Martyn Walsh and Anna Kathleen Walsh, *Plain English Handbook* (Cincinnati: McCormick Mathers Publishing Company, Inc., 1966), p. 61.

8. John C. Hodges, *Harbrace College Handbook* (New York: Harcourt, Brace and Company, 1951), p. 451.

9. Frank P. Adams, *Diagrams and Analyses* (Indianapolis: Normal Publishing House, 1886), p. 2.

10. Donald W. Emery, *Sentence Analysis* (New York: Holt, Rinehart and Winston, 1961), p. vi.

11. R. W. Pence and D. W. Emery, *A Grammar of Present-Day English* (New York: The Macmillan Company, 1963), p. 369.

words have one to another, and thereby facilitating grammatical exegesis, the cornerstone of theological exegesis.

DIAGRAMMATICAL ANALYSIS DESIGNED

Diagrammatical analysis has been a useful tool for students of grammar and rhetoric because it calls attention to word relationships within a sentence as it builds into paragraphs. "Obviously, the ability to diagram sentences does not automatically lead to skill in composing clear, correct, and graceful prose, any more than the ability to construct neat graphs and pie charts indicates a mastery of statistics."[12]

The individual who is unable to express in some graphic way the structure of sentences is frequently not able to grasp the complete thought housed in a group of words. On the other hand, students who are trained to chart the structure of visual thought patterns in the mechanics of sentence organization developing into wider thought patterns will have learned much regarding what the writer is endeavoring to communicate.

Various forms of diagramming have been employed over the years. Needless to say, any form is useful if it helps the analyst to understand the sentence. However, it must be kept in mind that "a diagram is only a means to an end, not an end in itself."[13]

A diagram for grammatical analysis is, then, nothing more than a map or chart that makes a subject easier to grasp in its entirety. A diagram in grammar bears about the same relationship to grammar that a map bears to geography, that a drawing of a piece of apparatus in a laboratory manual bears to chemistry, that a chart bears to some aspect of economics in a treatise on that subject. A diagram is ever a means of giving pictorial representation to analysis and is never an end in itself. Because it can reveal to the eye in one glance what the process of analysis is discovering, a diagram can have as much usefulness in the study of grammar as in the study of any other subject where analysis plays a leading role. In other words, there is nothing occult or hidden or mysterious about a diagram in grammar. It can be as simple and usable as a set of drawings telling one how to put together the separate parts to make a machine and then how to operate it.[14]

---

12. Emery, *Sentence Analysis,* p. vi.
13. Hodges, *Harbrace,* p. 452.
14. Pence and Emery, *Grammar,* pp. 369-70.

Diagrammatical analysis has four basic purposes: (1) it enables the interpreter to understand the structure of meaningful sentences contained in the Bible; (2) it enables the interpreter to structure a meaningful and workable outline whereby he can pass on God's truth to his hearers; (3) it enables the interpreter to observe the thought pattern of the biblical writer whom the Holy Spirit employed, and (4) it enables the interpreter to construct effective sentences of his own.

Howard Vos clearly declares:

Analysis to many means merely browsing through the text and stopping here and there to study or comment upon various words, phrases, or ideas. But such is not the case. In the first place, there must be an organized plan for any study of the message of the Word; second, there must be grammatical analysis of the text to discover accurately what that message is. . . . When the analysis is complete, the main lines of thought become clear, and the problem of outlining is simplified a great deal.[15]

The most obvious and simplest way of diagramming a sentence is to write the framework on a horizontal line—subject, verb, and object of the verb, and to write below this framework the words, phrases or clauses that modify them. Listen to Vos again as he sets forth a very honest and true-to-life observation;

In the development of this method there first must be grammatical analysis in which a study is made paragraph by paragraph with determination to discover the principle sentences and to note the grouping around them of subordinate sentences and clauses and the inter-relationships of these. Such a procedure is especially necessary in studying the Pauline epistles, in which the Apostle's constant deviations put the reader in danger of missing the main point of a passage under consideration. In reading a passage of Scripture hastily, it is easy to gain an erroneous impression as to its main theme. A grammatical diagram of the passage might demonstrate that what was considered to be the main theme actually appeared in a subordinate clause; it was not therefore the principal teaching at all.[16]

---

15. Howard F. Vos, *Effective Bible Study* (Grand Rapids: Zondervan Publishing House, 1956), p. 34.
16. Ibid., p. 33.

Such has been the testimony of many Bible expositors. What they thought was the teaching of a certain passage based on their own theological bias and a careful reading of the English text was not really what the text said after they laid it out in a grammatical diagram. Admittedly the grammatical analysis is not a 100% answer to all the problems one encounters in determining the exact message of any Scripture passage or text. However, if one is going to be an expositor of the Word, it is a *major step* in that direction. This step is vital in understanding the relationship of words and phrases to one another.

What is true of preparation to preach is also true of preaching. Grammatical analysis is definitely related to the subject of communication.

It is the goal of the seminary to enable each student to become the best possible preacher that he can possibly become. The seminary training is not viewed as terminal in the process of becoming a preacher. It is rather viewed as being the beginning which alerts the student to the proper procedures and practices which, if followed throughout life, will enable the preacher continuously to develop and to improve. As he goes through life the preacher should develop into a better and better preacher. This is true because preaching is an art which becomes polished by continuous and conscious practice.[17]

Diagrammatical analysis is a beginning tool, which if adhered to and followed throughout life, will enable the preacher to develop and improve his exegesis of the Word of God. This is what people need to hear and this is what many congregations are hearing for the first time as they sit under the ministry of a man of God who utilizes diagrammatical analysis in his sermonic preparation.

Let no student or preacher be misled into thinking that this is an easy task and that in diagrammatical analysis alone he will become a good preacher. No, it is work, hard work, often consuming long periods of time. But just as a preacher gets better with experience and becomes more polished by continuous and conscious practice, so the more one works with diagrammatical analysis, the more rewarding it is. After spending wearisome hours over a portion of the Scriptures, how encouraging it is to have a member of the congregation say after a fashion: "Pastor, you sure know how to teach and feed us the message of the Bible. Thank you."

---

17. Paul R. Fink, "A Design of the System and Facilities to be used in the Speech and Homiletics Program of Grace Theological Seminary, Winona Lake, Indiana." (Unpublished paper. The University of Southern California, July 1970), p. 3.

Testimonies are received expressing gratitude for the insistence upon a proper diagrammatical analysis of the Biblical text. Excerpts from two letters are included here. The first excerpt is from a pastor of a growing church (over 1300) in the Midwest.

> The growth number-wise at . . . has been fantastic to me. We grew 69% over the previous year. This is attributable to one fact only, that is the expository, systematic teaching of the Word. I have appreciated many times over the teaching and instruction I received . . . on how to get into the Word and dig into the richness of the Word, and then communicate the Word to those who would be under my ministry. Tools and techniques . . ., such as diagramming the text, are those that . . . have been invaluable in opening the Word to me and enabling me to teach it to others. As Christians are nourished on the Word, they have grown to further maturity and have carried on the work of the ministry, and that accounts for the growth in numbers. . . . Blessings of God on the work here as a result of the ministry of the Word are in a very real way a direct result of your ministry, and someday you will share in the rewards and it is only fitting that I should pass on to you something of what God has been doing here.

The second excerpt is from a pastor beginning a new church in the East.

> Last Sunday morning I preached to a group of 15 people—12 college students—on Phil. 2:5–11. I had faithfully diagrammed it out so I knew what the text said. So I sat in the group and expounded the Word for 45 minutes. During that time I could see some of the Christians nod their heads in *appreciation* not sleep! They grinned at times in complete enjoyment at knowing what the text meant. I was thinking during the sermon as I looked at those young people—"Hey!—I've got something to say—I know what this text means." That surge of confidence and certainty was worth it all. I just wanted you to know how I am using your teaching.
>
> One professor in the group has his Ph.D. in Latin, and follows along in the Greek N.T. I can see him at times nodding and saying—"Yes, yes—I see." . . . One of the girl students . . . said, "This is what I need—solid stuff."

Observation of what the Scripture text is communicating requires more than seeing or casual reading; it is scrutinizing and analyzing the data that the careful Bible student is endeavoring to interpret. If the interpreter is to gain a knowledge of the whole, he must first possess a knowledge of its particular parts. Then he must become saturated with the particulars of a passage so that he is thoroughly conscious of their existence, their relationship to each other and their required explanation. There is no such thing as an unimportant detail or word of the Scripture text. The interpreter must be exact with each detail in its morphology (form), lexicology (meaning) and syntax (relationship).

Doubly important is the grammatical relationship known as syntax, which is "the arrangement of words as elements in a sentence to show their relationship; sentence structure."[18] As syntax involves sentence structure, it is necessary to analyze the structural relations within the sentences. As the component parts of the sentence are analyzed and related to the whole, only then is one able to follow with assurance the Biblical writers train of thought. Thus, "syntax is a study of thought relations."[19]

> Exactness demands that the details are accurate; that is, present exactly that which the author intended to be presented. But regardless of how exact the details of a given passage might be, if they are incomplete, the researchers knowledge of the text will be incomplete. Therefore, a comprehensive knowledge of the passage is essential for an accurate understanding of its message.[20]

A study of syntactical relationships involves a consideration of context, which is defined as "the parts of a sentence, paragraph, discourse, etc. that occur just before and after a specified word or passage, and determine its exact meaning: . . . the whole situation, background, or environment relevant to some happening or personality."[21]

---

18. Noah Webster, *Webster's New Twentieth Century Dictionary of the English Language* (Cleveland: The World Publishing Company, 1971), p. 1852.
19. A. Berkeley Mickelsen, *Interpreting the Bible* (Grand Rapids: Wm. B. Eerdmans Publishing Company, 1963), p. 129.
20. Earl Marcus Bohnett, "Principles and Methods of Biblical Research" (Unpublished syllabus. Baptist Bible College, Denver, Colorado, February, 1966), p. 71.
21. Webster, *New Twentieth Century Dictionary,* p. 394.

Neglect of context is a common cause of erroneous interpretation and irrelevant application. . . . When interpretive applications are contrary to the context, many thinking readers lose confidence in all applications of that interpreter. Context is basic because it forces the interpreter to examine the entire line of thought of the writer. When the interpreter projects his own ideas into the thought he is interpreting, he ceases being an honest interpreter and becomes a personal propagandist under the guise of explaining the work of another.[22]

DIAGRAMMATICAL ANALYSIS DELINEATED

At this point, the purpose of this manual is brought into perspective. The object is threefold: (1) to define the parts of speech and to illustrate diagrammatical analysis in English so that the student may begin with a language with which he is familiar; (2) to illustrate the prominent features of diagrammatical analysis from the Hebrew and Greek texts which are individual languages all of their own; and (3) to show how diagrammatical analysis forms a basis for outlining the Biblical text in order to derive sermonic structure. This manual is not intended to be an exhaustive review of English grammar, nor of the grammatical features of the original languages of the Bible. It is a beginning tool upon which the interpreter can construct meaningful analyses of his own.

The portraiture used to represent grammatical relationships in sentences may vary slightly from book to book and teacher to teacher. How-ever, the flexible student who grasps the essential principles of diagramming will have little trouble with slight variations of style. *The following examples in no way exhaust the possibilities for variation in structure, but are intended only to "suggest the general pattern."*[23] It will be observed in the following examples that some sentences are not complete. The intention is to show how certain functions of sentence analysis should appear on a diagram so that sermonic structure is clearly discernable.

---

22. Mickelsen, *Interpreting the Bible,* pp. 99–100.
23. Robert F. Ramey, "Diagramming of Grammar," (Unpublished paper, Grace Theological Seminary, March 1971), p. 2.

No coach can teach strategy without some visual aid on which he diagrams his plays for his players to see. By the means of design, a player can view what every member of the team is doing when a select play is called. This same technique is used to help students master grammatical analysis. By means of a diagram, one can observe what every word of a sentence contributes to the understanding of the whole thought.[24]

> A diagram images the sentence. It meets the eye, stirs the imagination, objectifies the logic by visual impressions. Diagram dramatizes ideas, makes prominent what is prominent, subordinates what is dependent. It even points up any obscurities, ambiguities, or confusions in an author's thought. In spite of certain limitations diagramming remains a practical working tool for the expositor. If we would trace an author's thought we must retrace the author's thought. The discipline of the diagram offers the finest map available for guiding over the devious paths of the thinker whose thought has been put to paper.

This manual is *not* to be considered a complete handbook on grammar. The premise behind what follows is that the reader has studied basic English, Greek, and Hebrew grammar at some point in his educational experience. The Purpose is to develop one's understanding of the mechanics of diagramming. Therefore, the following visual aid section is crucial. "Important tips on diagramming" is as important as reading the instructions before putting together a child's toy or constructing some unfamiliar object. Happy graphics!

---

24. Crouch, *Expository Preaching and Teaching—Hebrews,* p. xxxviii.

IMPORTANT TIPS ON DIAGRAMMING

1. **Always write on the *horizontal base line*.** Ex. <u>God</u>

2. **Always clearly indicate proper sentence divisions by the use of *vertical lines* on the horizontal base line.**

Ex. <u>Subject | Verb | Direct Object</u>

3. **Always make all modifiers come off a single vertical line connected to the horizontal base line.** Always use a *solid line* to connect modifiers to the horizontal base line. Modifiers are to be placed on the subordinate horizontal line connected to the vertical line. Vertical lines are easier to follow than slanted lines in picking up sermonic outline structure.

Ex. <u>Subject | Verb | Direct Object</u>

4. **Always use *broken lines* to connect parallel horizontal base lines or thoughts.** It is more functional, but not mandatory, to connect the verbs by the use of broken lines with the conjunction or other transitional or connecting word(s) between the lines if such occurs in the text. The other possibility is to connect the beginning of each base line or thought with a broken line.

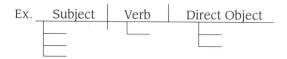

Ex. Subject | Verb | Direct Object

Conjunction   (or)

Subject | Verb \ Predicate Adjective

5. **Always place participles, infinitives and finite clauses on *stilts*.** This is not uniformly practiced by all exegetes, but if followed it will help the exegete to spot the functions of such grammatical constructions. In addition, it will help to facilitate the diagramming of attendant grammar which completes the sentence structure.

Ex.

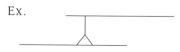

6. **Always diagram Greek like it is read—from left to right** (see following pages). The accents should be included with each word.

7. **Always diagram Hebrew like it is read—from right to left** (see following pages). Vowel pointings should be included with each word and are preferably placed below the horizontal line.

8. **In diagramming the main consideration is given to *function* not form.** However, the form is very important and must be considered. In Greek, the case endings will nearly always help the understanding of the function.

9. **Always diagram Hebrew and Greek words as a *single unit* according to the main function of the word.** In *Hebrew* do not separate prefixes, suffixes, prepositions, negatives, waw conjunction, words following the direct object sign or words connected by a maqqēph (hyphen-like line). In *Greek* do not separate prefixes, suffixes or negatives from their word association.

10. **Always place *parentheses* around words supplied to make the meaning clear or to fill in *ellipses*.**

Ex. Philippians 4:8
(ἐστὶν)

ὅσα	ἐστὶν	ἀληθῆ
ὅσα	(ἐστὶν)	σεμνά
ὅσα	(ἐστὶν)	δίκαια
ὅσα	(ἐστὶν)	ἁγνά
ὅσα	(ἐστὶν)	εὔφημα
ὅσα	(ἐστὶν)	προσφιλῆ

ἀδελφοί

λογίζεσθε | ταῦτα ↔

11. **Always put *transitional words* relating to preceding context in upper left hand corner in Greek; in Hebrew place such words in upper right hand corner.** This should be done only if such words occur in the first verse of the diagrammed text. Otherwise verses should be connected together with broken lines as previously mentioned in point 4 above.

Ex.   And   (Greek)   (Hebrew)   But

Subject | Verb   Verb | Subject

12. **It is extremely important that the interpreter *be able to iden-tify the various grammatical terms.*** If the interpreter cannot identify the various terms, then he cannot place them in their proper order; which will result in his inability to understand their intended meaning within the syntax. (Bohnett, p. 75). Terms may be identified according to the following grammatical categories: nouns, pronouns, verbs, adjectives, adverbs, participles, infinitives, prepositions, conjunctions, imperatives, articles, and interjections. In addition, the interpreter should be familiar with other grammatical terms such as: subject, predicate, direct object, indirect object, predicate nominative, predicate adjective, apposition, phrase, clause, antecedent, and modifier. These are only a few of the many grammatical terms used in language. The interpreter should be aware of these and others and know where to gain help in clarifying his understanding of the multitude of grammatical terms. To be able to identify the various terms alone is insufficient. The interpreter must be able to notice their inflectional forms and identify the declension and case of each substantive as to gender, number and case. Also, he must be able to conjugate the verbs as to tense, mood, person and number. Once all the various terms are distinguished, their syntactical relationships can be constructed.

13. **Always use the following analysis of the *vertical and slanted lines* as they touch the horizontal base line to indicate the sentence divisions and/or parts of speech.** Notice the *only* vertical line drawn *through* the main/base line is that which divides the subject and the verb. All other vertical and slanted lines meet but do not extend through the horizontal base line.

Subject	Verb

Verb	Direct Object

/ Indirect Object   (or)

	Indirect Object

\ Predicate Adjective, Objective Complement, etc.

Preposition	Object of Preposition

Note: When a star (*) appears on the following pages of the diagram, it is there to draw attention to the function under consideration.

CHAPTER ONE

Basic Illustrative Diagram Patterns

SENTENCE ANALYSIS

A. *Simple Sentence*—A clause containing a subject and a finite verb.

   1. *Subject and Predicate*

      Subject—That of which something is said (a noun or noun equivalent).

      Predicate—That which is said of the subject (contains the verb, adverbial modifiers, and complements).

The subject may be a noun.

     John 1:28   John | was baptizing

The subject may be a personal pronoun.

     John 1:20   He | confessed

The subject may be a relative pronoun.

     John 1:13   Who | were born

The subject may be an indefinite pronoun.

     John 10:42   Many | believed

The subject may be a demonstrative pronoun.

John 20:31 <u>These | are written</u>

John 11:35 "Jesus wept."

Genesis 1:1 "God created."

John 3:2 "This one came"

Exodus 3:14 "I AM has sent me"

2. *Subject, Predicate, Direct Object and Objective Complement*

Direct Object—The receiver (noun or noun equivalent) of the action of the predicate (verb), i.e. the transitive verb.

Objective Complement—That which renames or describes a direct object.

The direct object may be a noun.

John 3:16 <u>God | loved | world</u>
                   so   the

The direct object may be a personal pronoun.

John 7:44   Some | would have taken | him

The direct object may be a relative pronoun.

the men

John 17:6   Thou | gavest | whom

me

The direct object may be an indefinite pronoun.

John 5:30   I | can do | nothing

The direct object may be a demonstrative pronoun.

John 7:39   He | spoke | this

The objective complement is adjectival in function.

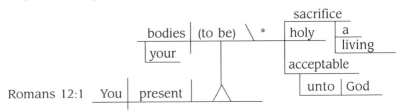

Romans 12:1   "Therefore brethren, I beseech you ... to present your bodies a living sacrifice holy, well pleasing to God."

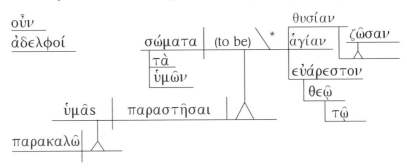

John 11:5 "Jesus loved Martha"

Genesis 1:1 "God created the heavens"

אֱלֹהִים | בָּרָא | * אֵת הַשָּׁמַיִם

3. *Subject, Predicate and Indirect object*

> *Indirect Object*—Designates the person to whom or for whom, or the thing to which or for which, the action of the verb is performed.

An indirect object may be a noun or one of the classes of pronouns.

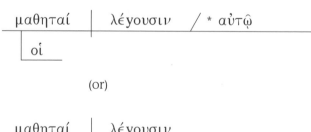

(or)

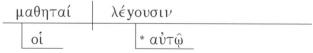

John 11:8 "The disciples said to him"

μαθηταί | λέγουσιν / * αὐτῷ
οἱ

(or)

μαθηταί | λέγουσιν
οἱ | * αὐτῷ

Genesis 37:13 "And Israel said to Joseph"

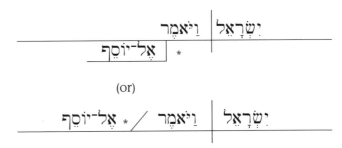

(or)

4. *Subject, Predicate and Subjective Complement, Predicate Nominative or Predicate Adjective*

Subject Complement, Predicate Nominative, or Predicate Adjective (Predicate noun or pronoun)—The sentence unit which is joined to the subject by a linking verb and renames or describes the subject.

John 17:3 This | is * life
                        | eternal

John 1:14 "The Word became flesh"

λόγος | ἐγένετο * σάρξ
    ὁ

Genesis 42:6 "And Joseph, he was the ruler"

הַשַּׁלִּיט */ (was) | הוּא ↔ וְיוֹסֵף

5. *Nouns in Apposition* - (⟵——⟶)

> *Appositive*—A noun unit (word, phrase, or clause) placed next to
> another noun to restate or rename it. Both expressions
> must have the same grammatical construction.

I Peter 5:8

Adversary ↔ devil	walks about

the   the

of | you

I Peter 5:8 "The adversary of you the devil walks about ..."

ἀντίδικος ↔ διάβολος | περιπατεῖ

ὁ

ὑμῶυ

Philippians 4:15 "You Philippians know"

ὑμεῖς ↔ φιλιππήσιοι | οἴδατε

Genesis 42:4 "And Benjamin, the brother of Joseph, Jacob
did not send."

אֲחִי ↔ וְאֶת־בִּנְיָמִין | לֹא־שָׁלַח | יַעֲקֹב

יוֹסֵף

6. *Adjectival and Adverbial Modifiers*

> *Modifier*—A word or group of words that changes or describes the
> meaning of another word.
>
> *Adjective*—Words which add to the meaning of a noun by
> describing or limiting or identifying it.
>
> *Adverb*—A word, phrase, or clause used to modify a verb, an
> adjective, or another adverb.

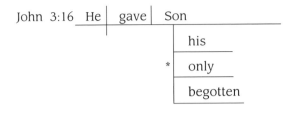

John 3:16

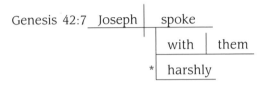

Genesis 42:7

John 10:11   "I am the good shepherd"

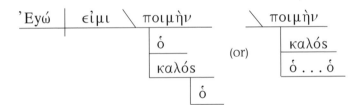

(or)

Second attributive position: article with adjective really modifies noun

Philippians 2:12   "My beloved, work out as always you obeyed, the salvation of yourselves."

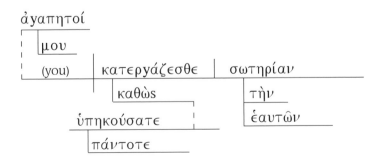

Genesis 1:2 "And the Spirit of God moved upon the face of the waters."

Genesis 42:7 "And Joseph spoke with them harshly."

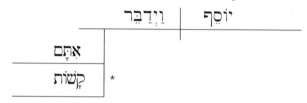

7. Prepositional Phrase

Preposition—A word which ties a following noun (or noun equivalent), called its object, to some other sentence unit. It shows the relationship between the two. The preposition and its object constitute a prepositional phrase.

Ephesians 1:1 Paul ↔ apostle

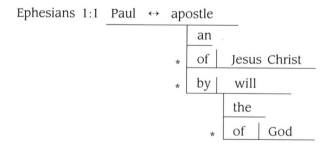

John 10:11 "The good shepherd lays down for the sheep, his life."

Philippians 4:6 "Your requests let be made known in
everything by prayer and supplication
with thanksgivings to God."

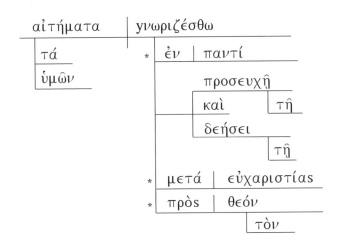

Genesis 1:1 "God created in the beginning"

אֱלֹהִים | בָּרָא
בְּרֵאשִׁית | *

Genesis 37:29 "And Reuben returned unto the pit"

רְאוּבֵן | וַיָּשָׁב
אֶל־הַבּוֹר | *

Genesis 37:14 "And he sent him from the valley of
Hebron and he came to Shechem."

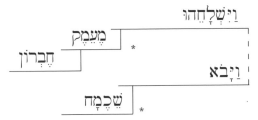

B. *Compound Subjects, Verbs, Objects and Modifiers*

1. *Compound Subjects—*(Two or more simple subjects)

John 1:17

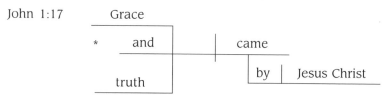

Matthew 15:1 "Pharisees and scribes approached Jesus from Jerusalem then"

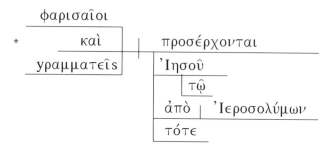

Genesis 44:14 "And Judah and his brothers came to the house of Joseph."

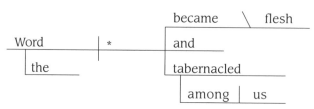

2. *Compound Verbs—(Two or more simple verbs)*

John 1:14

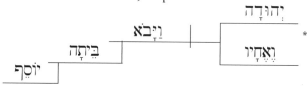

John 1:14   "The Word became flesh and tabernacled among us."

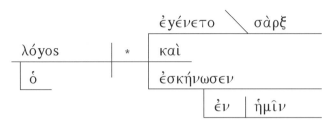

Genesis 37:5   "Joseph dreamed a dream and he told (it) to his brothers."

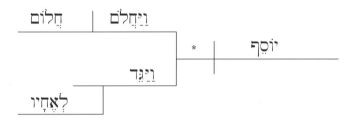

3. *Compound Objects*—(Two or more simple objects)

John 11:5

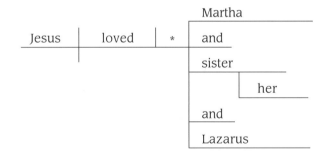

Genesis 1:1–2

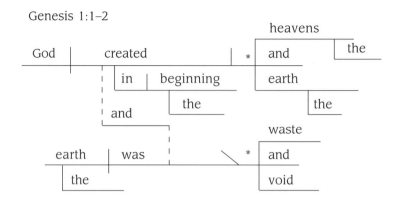

John 11:5 "Jesus loved Martha and her sister and Lazarus."

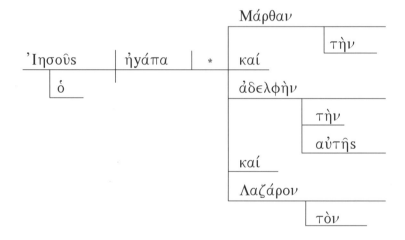

Genesis 1:1–2 "God created in the beginning the heavens and the earth and the earth was waste and void."

4. *Compound Modifiers*—(Two or more simple modifiers)

Titus 2:12

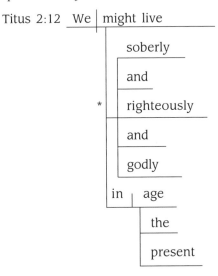

Titus 2:12 "We might live soberly and righteously and godly in the now (present) age."

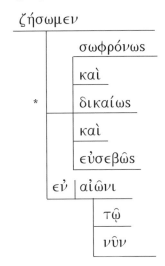

Genesis 1:14 "And God said let there be lights in the firmament of the heavens to divide between the day and between the night; and let them be for signs, and for seasons, and for days and years."

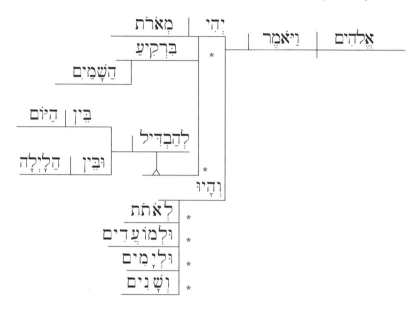

C. *Compound Sentence*—(Two or more simple sentences connected by a conjunctive word, by words, or by punctuation; called independent clauses when used as a single sentence.)

Independent clause—See following point D.

John 4:38b

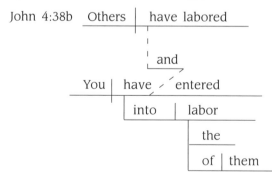

John 4:38b "Others have labored and you have entered into the labor of them."

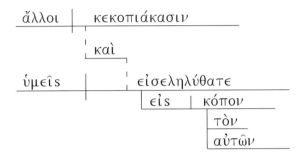

James 4:10 "You be humbled before (the) Lord and he will exalt you."

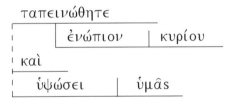

Genesis 22:3 "And Abraham rose up early in the morning, and saddled his donkey, and took two of his lads (young men) with him and Isaac his son; and he cut the wood for a burnt-offering, and rose up and went to the place of which God said to him."

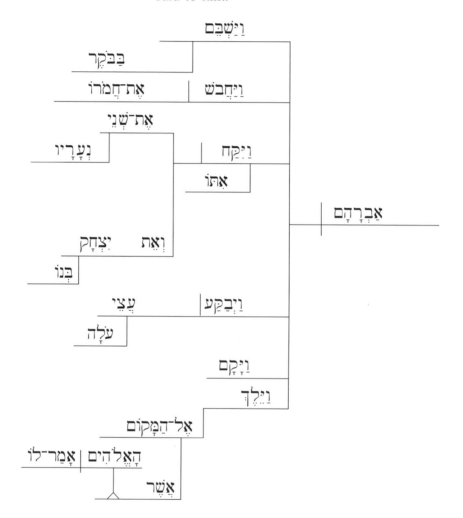

D. *Complex Sentence* (one independent and one or more dependent clauses)

> *Independent Clause*—A simple sentence containing no conjunctive word to make it dependent upon another clause.
>
> *Dependent* (subordinate) *Clause*—Contains an expressed or implied conjunctive word that keeps the clause from functioning satisfactorily as a complete statement. Dependent clauses also function as nouns, adjectives, or adverbs.

Genesis 41:57

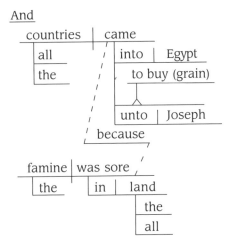

John 11:6

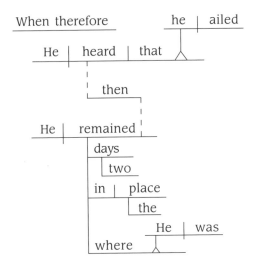

John 11:6 "When therefore He heard that he ailed, then he remained, in which he was, place, two days."

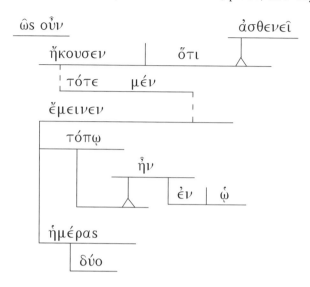

Genesis 41:57 "And all the countries came into Egypt to buy (grain) unto Joseph, because the famine was sore (strong) in all the land."

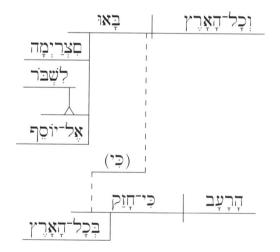

E. *Sentence Function*

1. *Declarative Sentence (makes a statement)*

John 3:14   "Moses | lifted | serpent

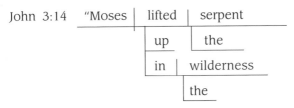

John 3:14   "Moses lifted up in the wilderness the serpent."

Genesis 42:21   "We are truly guilty concerning our brother"

2. *Interrogative Sentence (asks a question)*

Romans 8:35   Who | shall separate | us

John 19:15   "Shall I crucify your king?"

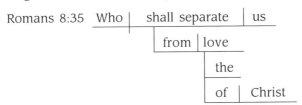

John 1:19   "Who are you?"

Genesis 40:8   "Do not interpretations belong to God?"

Genesis 42:28   "What is this, God has done unto us?"

3. *Imperative Sentence* (Expresses a command or an entreaty)

I Thessalonians 5:19

Ephesians 5:1   Therefore

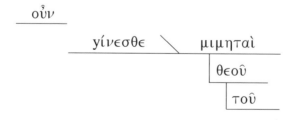

Matthew 2:13   "You take the child and his mother and flee
into Egypt."

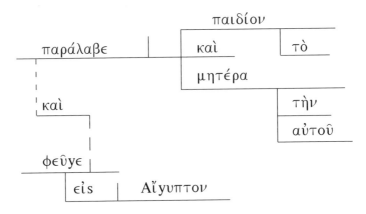

Genesis 37:22   "Throw him into the pit"

Genesis 37:27   "Come and we will sell him to the
Ishmaelites."

Psalm 34:11   "Come, sons, listen to me! I will teach you the
fear of Jehovah."

4. *Exclamatory Sentence* (Expresses surprise or strong emotion)

Romans 7:24

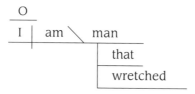

Romans 7:24   "O wretched man that I am!"

τὰλαίπωρος ⟷ ἄνθρωπος

(that)

ἐγὼ

Deuteronomy 28:67

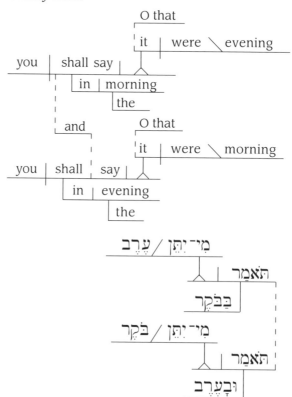

PHRASE ANALYSIS

Phrase—A Group of related words which does not contain a subject and a finite verb (predicate) in combination, and which functions within a larger unit as a substantive, as a modifier, or as an independent unit.

A. *Nominative Phrase* (Mostly used with participles and/or infinitives in this position)

Matthew 28:15

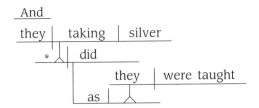

Matthew 28:15   "And they taking silver did as they were taught."

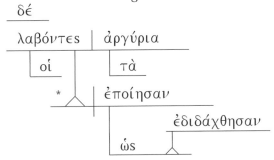

Genesis 38:25   "She was brought forth and she sent to her father-in-law saying . . ."

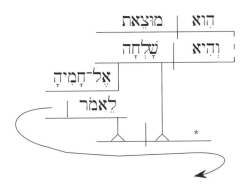

B. *Objective Phrase* (Mostly used with participles and/or infinitives in this position)

3 John 8

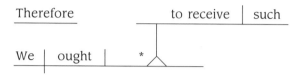

3 John 8 "Therefore, we ought to receive such, that fellow workers we may be with the truth."

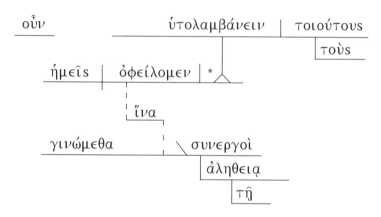

3 John 12c "Thou knowest that the witness of us is true."

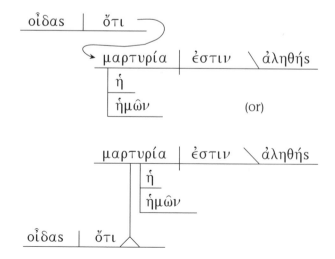

Genesis 37:6 "And he said unto them, listen now (to) this
dream which I have dreamed."

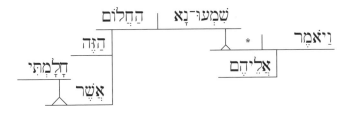

C. *Prepositional Phrase* (cf. Simple Sentence, point 7)

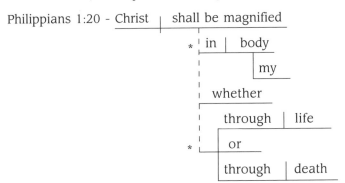

Philippians 1:20 - "Christ shall be magnified now in my
body whether through life or through
death."

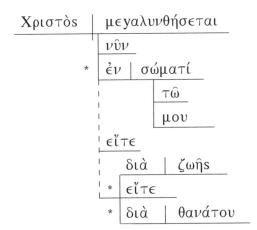

Genesis 42:2   "And he said, behold, I heard that there is food in Egypt, go down there and obtain for us from there and we shall live and not die."

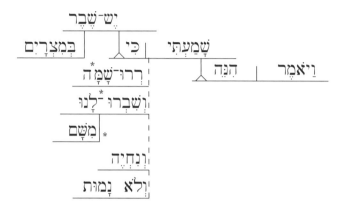

D. *Participle Phrase*

Participle (gerund)—A nonfinite verb form identified by any --ing ending and used in a noun position but called a verbal adjective: i.e., it is a form of a verb (may take an object) used as an adjective to modify a noun or a pronoun.

1. *As a modifier*

   a. *Adjectival participle*

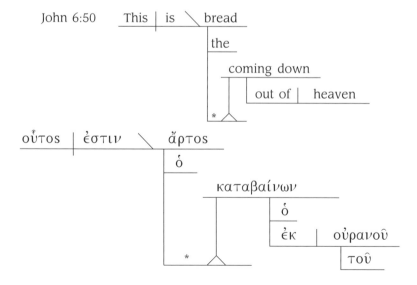

b. *Adverbial participle*

Matthew 3:1

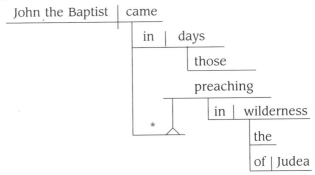

Matthew 3:1 "John the Baptist appeared in the wilderness of Judea."

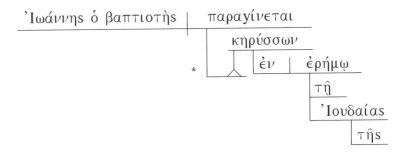

Genesis 45:1a "And Joseph was not able to restrain himself before all the ones standing about him . . ."

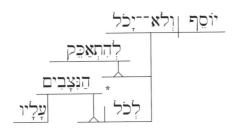

2. *As a Subject*

John 3:29

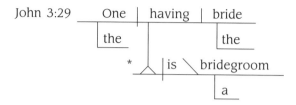

John 3:29 "The one having the bride is a bridegroom."

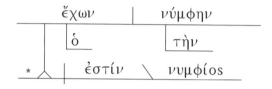

Genesis 37:25 ". . . and their camels carrying spice, balsam and myrrh going to bring down to Egypt."

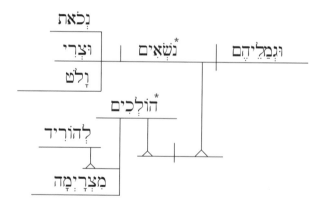

3. *As a Verb*

Genesis 37:7

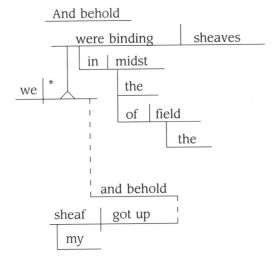

Philippians 3:4 ". . . I am having trust in the flesh also."

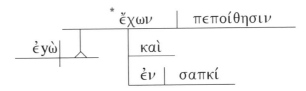

Genesis 37:7 "And behold we were binding sheaves in the midst of the field and behold my sheaf got (rose) up."

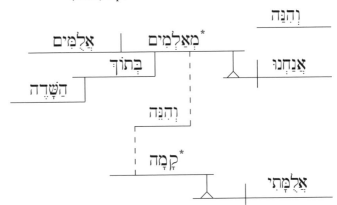

4. *As a Predicate Adjective or Direct Object*

Genesis 42:9

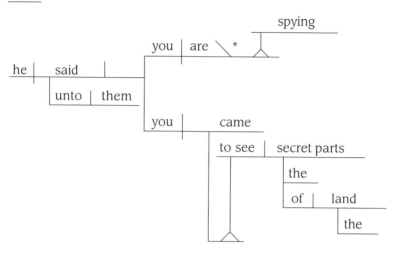

Philippians 2:13 "God is the one operating in you both to will and to operate on behalf of his goodwill."

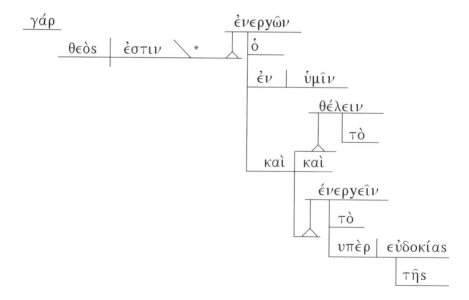

Genesis 42:9   "And he said, unto them, you are spying, you came to see the secret parts of the land."

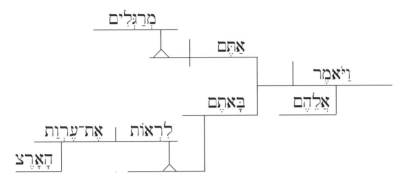

E. *Infinitive Phrase*

Infinitive—A form of a verb introduced normally (not always) by the sign "to"; called a verbal noun, and used as a noun, an adjective, or an adverb.

1. *As Subject of the Verb*

Romans 7:18   For

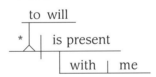

Philippians 1:21   "For to live (is) Christ and to die (is) gain to me."

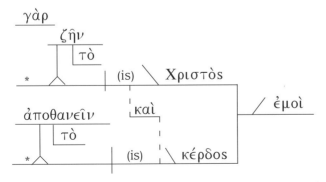

2. As Direct Object of the Verb

Mark 12:12 <u>And</u>

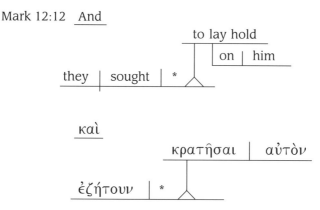

Philippians 2:6 "Who subsisting in the form of God, deemed it not robbery to be equal with God."

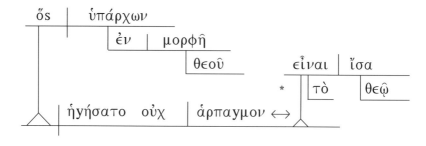

3. As a Verb

Matthew 2:2 <u>And</u>

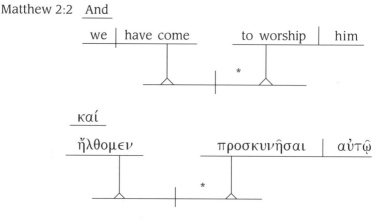

4. *As a Modifier*

John 1:12

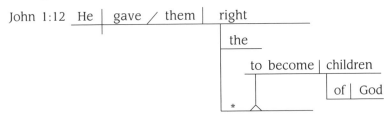

Romans 1:28 "God gave up them to a reprobate mind, to do the things not (being) proper."

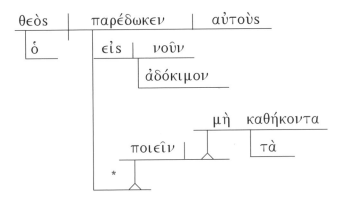

5. *Usage in Indirect Discourse*

Matthew 16:13

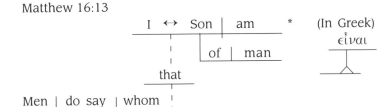

Matthew 16:13 "Whom do men say that I the Son of man am?"

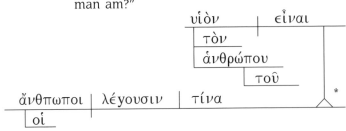

I Samuel 10:16 "And Saul said to his uncle, he told plainly that she-asses were found."

6. *The infinitive absolute* (peculiar to Hebrew). Expresses emphasis when it immediately precedes the finite verb, and duration when it immediately follows the finite verb.

Genesis 43:7 "And they said, the man inquired closely about us and about our family."

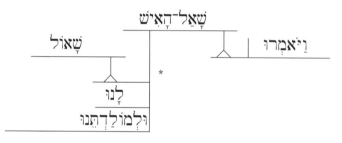

7. *The infinitive construct* (peculiar to Hebrew). With the preposition לְ expresses the English infinitive "to"

Genesis 37:18 "And they deceitfully plotted against him to put him to death."

Genesis 37:5 "And they continued more to hate him."

CLAUSE ANALYSIS

Clause—A group of words which contains a subject and a predicate (verb). It is usually considered a part of a sentence; but when it is capable of standing alone, it is equivalent to a simple sentence.

A. *Relative Clause*—Generally considered a subordinate clause that is introduced by a relative pronoun, adjective or adverb and relates (modifies) an antecedent. However it functions in various ways and is either definite or indefinite. It contains a word by means of which the complete expression of one idea is connected in sense with the complete expression of another.

Matthew 10:38

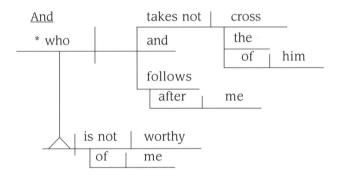

Matthew 10:38 - "And (he) who takes not the cross of him and follows after me, is not of me worthy."

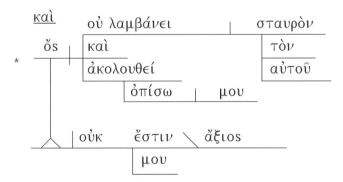

John 12:1   "Jesus came to Bethany where was Lazarus whom Jesus raised from the dead."

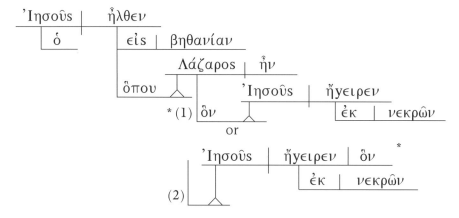

Suggestions:

For clarification of function and case of the relative pronoun use:

Example (1)—for Genitive and Dative cases.

Example (2)—for Nominative (properly placed in subject position) and Accusative cases.

Genesis 37:6   "Listen now (to) this dream which I have dreamed."

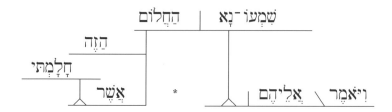

Clauses in Hebrew, regardless of classification, are diagrammed according to one of the following patterns, which are similar to the Greek pattern. Variation will occur according to the peculiar Hebrew syntax of the analyzed text. The only exception is the conditional clause which is generally referred to as the conditional sentence (See point H).

Genesis 44:24   "And it came to pass, we told to him the words of my lord, when we went up to your servant, my father."

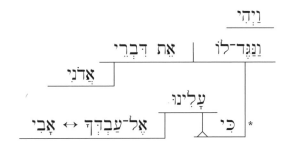

Genesis 4:8   ". . . And Cain rose up against Abel his brother and killed him, as they were in the field."

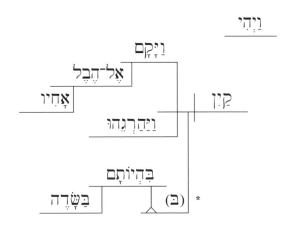

NOTE: The preposition is placed in parentheses to aid recognition and understanding. For students with a good grasp of Hebrew this can be omitted.

B. *Temporal Clause*—Function is to limit the action of the verb in the principle clause by the introduction of a relation of time.

Matthew 7:28

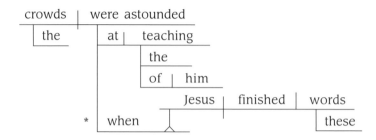

Matthew 7:28 "And it came to pass, the crowds were astounded at the teaching of him, when Jesus finished these words."

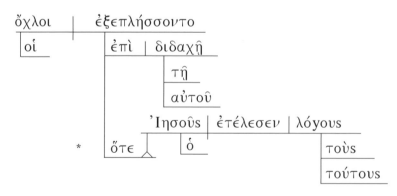

C. *Local Clause*—Introduced by a relative adverb of place.

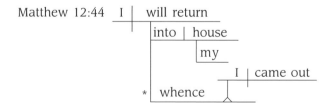

Matthew 12:44   "I will return into my house whence I came out."

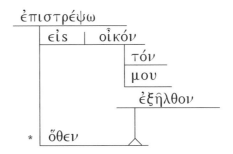

D. *Subordinating Clause*—Dependent upon the main clause and used as a part of speech in the sentence but usually does not make sense when standing alone.

I Corinthians 11:2

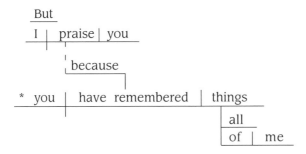

I Corinthians 11:2   "But I praise you because you have remembered all things of me."

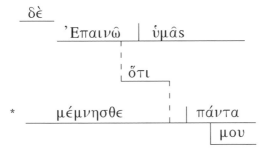

John 14:19 "Also, you will live because I live."

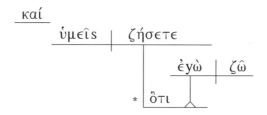

Genesis 43:18 - "And the men were afraid because they were brought to the house of Joseph."

E. *Purpose and Result Clauses*

> *Purpose Clause*—Function is to express the aim of the action denoted by the main verb.

> *Result Clause*—States that which is consequent upon or issues from the action of the main verb.

John 10:38

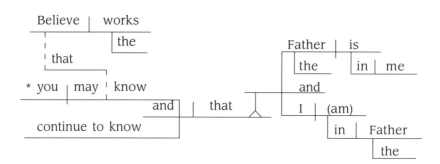

John 10:38 "Believe the works, that you may know and continue to know that the Father is in me and I in the Father."

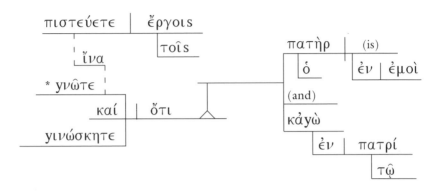

F. *Comparative Clause*—Introduces an analogous thought for the purpose of elucidating or emphasizing the thought expressed in the principle clause.

Hebrews 4:2

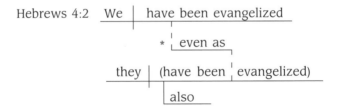

Hebrews 4:2 "For indeed, we have had the glad tidings announced, even as they also."

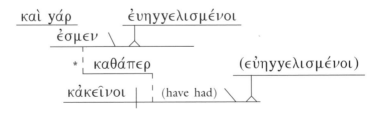

G. *Concessive Clause*—Essentially these clauses are conditional in nature. They differ, however, in that the apodosis attains reality by reason of the protasis of the conditional clause, while in the concessive clause realization is secured in spite of the protasis.

John 8:16 <u>But</u>

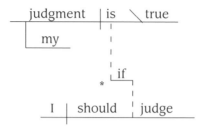

John 8:16 "And if I judge also, my judgment is true."

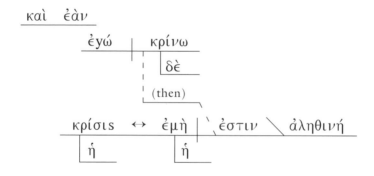

II Corinthians 7:8 "Because if I indeed grieved you by the epistle, (then) I do not regret (it).

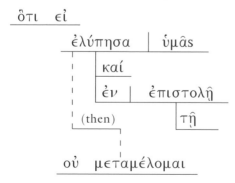

H. *Conditional Clauses*—Statements of a supposition, the fulfillment of which is assumed to secure the realization of a potential fact expressed in a companion clause. The clause containing the supposition is called the protasis. The clause containing the statement based on the supposition is called the apodosis. Conditional clauses may be classified on the basis of the attitude they express with reference to reality.

1. *The Simple Condition*—This condition is used when one wishes to assume or seems to assume the reality of his premise. This is also called a first class conditional sentence or the condition determined as fulfilled.

Galatians 5:18 But if (since)

you | are led

by | Spirit

the

(then)

you | are not

under | law

Galatians 5:18 "But if you are led by the Spirit (then) you are not under law."

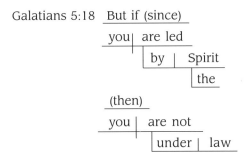

Job 10:14 If

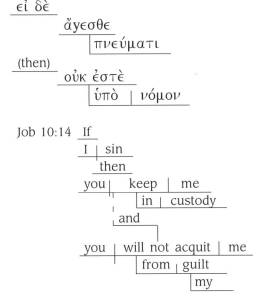

Job 10:14   "If I (indeed) sin, then you keep me in custody and you will not acquit me from my guilt."

2. *The Contrary to Fact Condition*—The premise is assumed to be contrary to fact, and only the past tenses of the indicative are used. The thing in itself may be true, but it is treated as untrue. The condition has only to do with the statement, not with the actual fact. This is also called a second-class conditional sentence or the condition determined as unfulfilled.

John 11:32

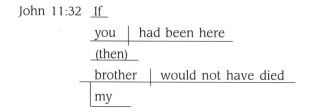

John 11:32   "If you had been here, (then) my brother would not have died."

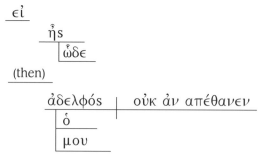

Isaiah 1:9  Except

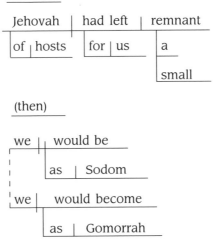

Jehovah	had left	remnant
of hosts	for us	a
		small

(then)

we | would be

as | Sodom

we | would become

as | Gomorrah

Isaiah 1:9 "Except Jehovah of hosts had left for us a few sur-
vivors, (then) we would be as Sodom, we would
become as Gomorrah."

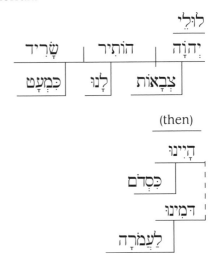

3. *The More Probable Future Condition*—Uncertainty is implied. This is also called the third class conditional sentence or the condition undetermined, but with prospect of determination.

1 John 1:8 If

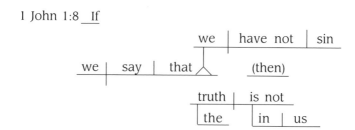

1 John 1:8 "If we should say that we have not sin, (then) we deceive ourselves, and the truth is not in us."

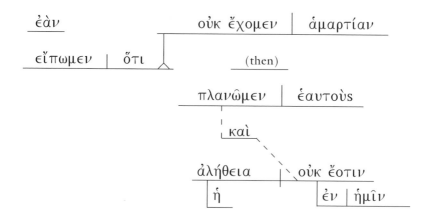

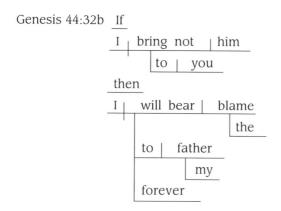

Genesis 44:32b "If I do not bring him back to you, then I will
be a sinner against my father all the days."

4. *The Less Probable Future Condition*—This is called the fourth
class condition or the condition undetermined and with re-
mote prospect of determination. In the New Testament no
whole example of this class of condition occurs. There is
found the condition (protasis) or the conclusion (apodosis),
but not both at the same time.

1 Peter 3:14

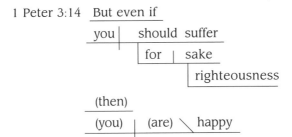

1 Peter 3:14   "But even if you should also suffer on account of righteousness, (then) you are blessed."

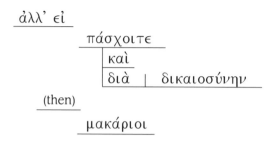

Genesis 13:16b   If

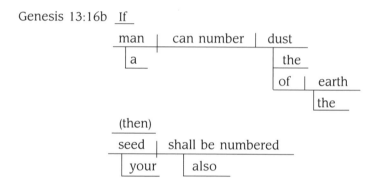

Genesis 13:16b   "If a man is able to count the dust of the earth, (then) also your seed will be counted."

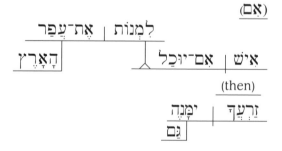

I. *Clause-al Connectives* - Clause-al connectives may be expressed either by a term or a prepositional phrase. They are divided into four categories—temporal or chronological, local or geographical, logical, and emphatic.[1]

    (a)   <u>Temporal or chronological connectives.</u>

after	John 3:22
as	John 9:1
before	John 8:58
now	John 4:42
then	John 7:10
until	John 9:18
when	John 2:23
while	John 5:7

    (b)   <u>Local or geographical connectives.</u>

at	John 20:12
beyond	John 1:28
in	John 15:4
near	John 3:23
on	John 19:37
over	John 18:1
there	John 14:3
unto	John 19:17
where	John 20:2
wherein	John 19:41

    (c)   <u>Logical connectives.</u>

Reason -

because	John 6:41
for	John 9:22
in that	John 9:17
that	John 8:22

---

1. Taken from Robert Traina's *Methodical Bible Study* (pp. 42–43) by Earl. M. Bohnett, "Principles and Methods of Biblical Research," pp. 83–86.

Result -

so	John 3:8
then	Matthew 24:14
therefore	John 20:20
thus	Romans 10:6

Purpose -

that	John 3:16

Contrast -

although	John 4:2
but	John 3:36
much more	Romans 5:15
nevertheless	John 16:7
otherwise	I Corinthians 14:16
yet	John 6:36

Comparison -

as	John 7:38
as - so	John 15:4
even as	John 17:14
even so	John 5:26
likewise	Romans 1:27

Series of Facts -

and	John 1:14

Any of the above connectives can be used in this manner.

first of all	I Timothy 2:1
last of all	I Corinthians 15:8
or	II Corinthians 6:15

Condition -

if	John 13:35

(d)   Emphatic connectives.

indeed	John 8:36
only	John 13:9
truly	John 8:31
verily	I John 2:5

It should be noted, first of all, that the same connectives may be found in more than one category. As an example, you will note that the temporal connectives may also be employed as a logical connective.

Second, many of these same relations are operative within a clause as well as between clauses. Those connectives which involve comparison, such as similes and metaphors, are excellent examples (see the parables in Matthew 13).

Last, sometimes the relation between clauses and sentences is implicit rather than explicit. The connective may not be expressed, and, therefore, the relations will have to be derived from the thoughts expressed or from the comparative position of the clauses or sentences in question (see John 14:17).

SPECIALIZED ANALYSIS

A. *Vocative*—Direct address: A grammatical construction by which a word or phrase indicates a person or group of people to whom is spoken what follows in the sentence.

Galatians 3:1

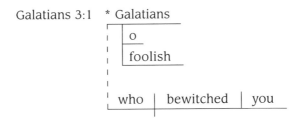

Galatians 3:1   "O foolish Galatians, who bewitched you"

Hosea 14:1 "O Israel, return unto Jehovah your God, because (for) you have stumbled by your iniquity."

B. *Conjunctions*—A conjunction is a word that connects sentences, clauses, phrases, and words. It may be a mere colorless copulative giving no additional meaning to the words preceding or following, or it may introduce a new meaning in addition to being a connective. These are also called transitional words.

John 3:17

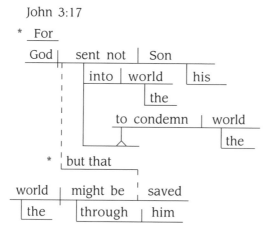

Matthew 5:43   "You shall love your neighbor and hate your enemy"

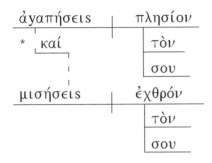

Matthew 4:4 - ". . . man shall not live only on bread but on every word . . ."

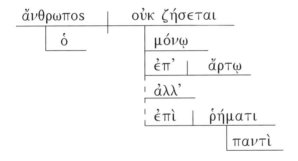

The most common Hebrew conjunction is the <u>waw</u>. It is attached mainly to verbs or nouns, and frequently to other parts of speech. However, it is never separated from its word-unit in the Biblical text and neither is it necessary in the diagram of the text. When the <u>waw</u> coordinates verbs, nouns, phrases and clauses, the diagram takes accordingly the form of compound verbs, compound nouns, compound phrases and compound or complex sentences. The <u>waw</u> conjunction differs in form before various word beginnings and has a wide usage. Many examples are evident on the preceding pages of this manual. While the foremost meaning of the <u>waw</u> conjunction is "and," context alone will determine the translation which is most appropriate. Other Hebrew terms function as conjunctions, but they may also function as prepositions and demonstrative particles introducing objective or adverbial clauses. Neither the <u>waw</u> conjunction nor any Hebrew word functioning as a connecting word can be characterized by any one diagrammatical form. Contextual usage is always the preeminent consideration.

Genesis 42:2   ". . . go down there and obtain (grain) for us from there in order that we may live and not die."

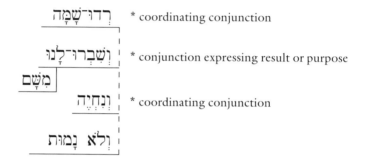

* coordinating conjunction

* conjunction expressing result or purpose

* coordinating conjunction

Genesis 42:10   "And they said to him, No, my lord, the fact is (rather, but), your servants have come to purchase food."

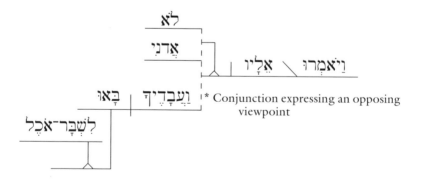

* Conjunction expressing an opposing viewpoint

Genesis 12:13 "Please say, that you are my sister so that it may be well with me because of you . . ."

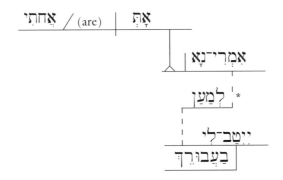

C. *Indirect Discourse*—Indirect declarations, indirect questions, and indirect commands. A statement of a person without quoting his/her exact words. Example: "He said that he would be there." Comparatively, an example of direct discourse is: "He said, I will be there." Diagrammatical analysis will vary according to context and syntax. Sentences are normally turned around and general patterns are as follows:

John 11:27 "I believe that you are the Christ."

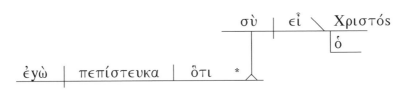

John 11:27

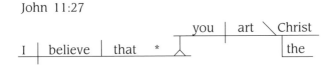

Genesis 12:12-13 ". . . then they will say, this is his wife . . .
please say that you are my sister . . ."

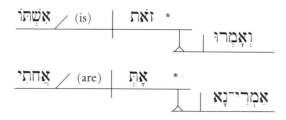

D. *Nominative Absolute* or *Independent Nominative*—When an idea is conceived independent of any verbal relations, the expression of it may be left standing alone in the nominative with some descriptive or explanatory phrase added. Names an idea rather than an object.

2 Peter 3:3 "I stir up . . . knowing first this, that mockers will come during the close of the days in mocking going . . . saying . . ."

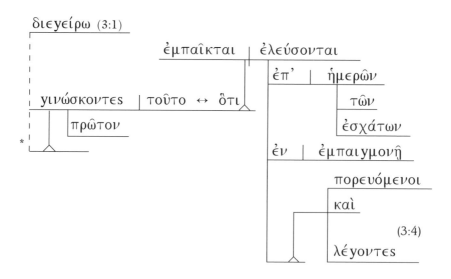

Luke 21:6   "You behold these things, the day in which . . . will come."

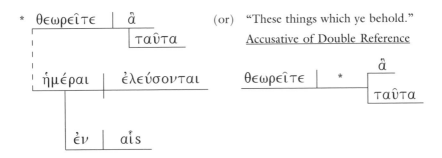

E. *Genitive Absolute*—A noun and a participle in the genitive case not grammatically connected with the rest of the sentence.

Matthew 9:33   "And the dumb man spoke, the demon having been cast out."

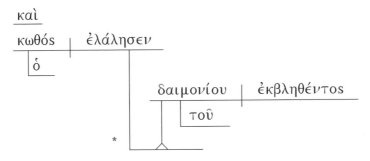

Matthew 14:32   "And the wind ceased, having entered into the ship."

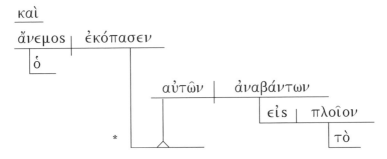

F. *Double Accusative*—More than one object is required to complete verbal meaning, i.e. many verbs and forms of verbs govern two or more objects.

John 14:26   "That one will teach you all things."

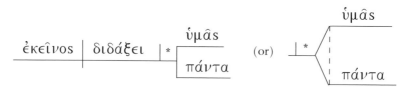

Genesis 42:25   ". . . and they filled their vessels (with) grain . . ."

Deuteronomy 8:3   ". . . and He caused you to eat the manna . . . "

G. *Adverbial Accusative of Reference*—The accusative used as the subject of the infinitive is called an accusative of reference.

> Ephesians 1:4 "As He chose us in Him before the foundation of the world, that we should be holy and unblemished before Him, in love predestinating . . ."

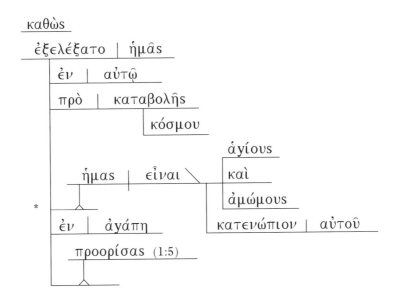

H. *Modifier(s) of Compound Units*—The modifier(s) equally changes or describes each word in the compound unit. The modifiers may be single terms, phrases or clauses. Hebrew is diagrammed the same, only the opposite way as it is read.

> Hebrews 12:1–2 ". . . let us run . . . fixing our eyes upon the author and perfecter of faith . . ."

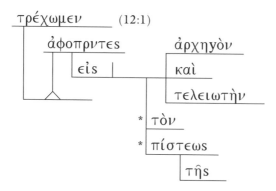

I. *Single Negative with Compound Verbs*—Occurs when intervening words are between the negative and the verbs, and the negative is not attached to another term by a maqqeph in Hebrew. The same possibility in Greek is diagrammed the opposite way, as it is read.

> Deuteronomy 7:7 "Jehovah did not love (attach himself to) you or choose you . . ."

J.   *The Particles* μέν δέ—All emphatic particles emphasize some word in a sentence or the thought of the sentence as a whole.

Jude 8   "Likewise indeed also, these (the) dreaming ones on the one hand defile the flesh but on the other hand despise lordship, and speak evil of the glories."

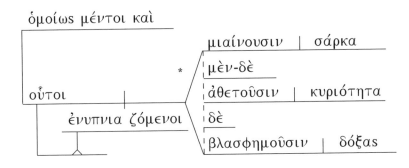

Jude 10   "But these on the one hand speak evil of what things they know not; on the other hand they are corrupted by these things which they understand naturally as animals without reason."

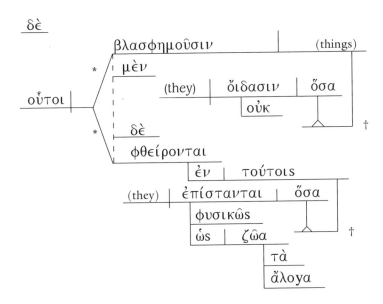

Note: Diagramming modifiers to the left(†) is only a space saving factor, it has no grammatical or interpretive significance.

K. *Complementary Infinitive*—completes the meaning of certain verbs such as "ought" (2 Cor. 12:11), "love" (Mt. 6:5), "wish" (Mk. 12:38), "able" (Mt. 9:28), and "about" (Mt. 11:14). The completed meaning is: "ought to have commanded," "love to pray," "wish to walk," "able to do," and "about to come." Similar English expressions are: "want to go," "love to sell," "ought to buy," "wish to see," etc.

> Ephesians 5:28   "The husbands so ought to love the wives of themselves as the bodies of themselves."

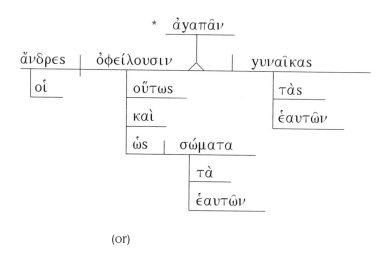

(or)

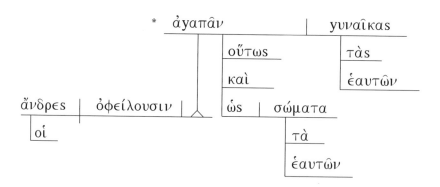

The Hebrew infinitive construct occurs in a wide variety of complementary uses often with the meaning of purpose, goal or result. A sequence of two infinitive absolutes often complements a finite verb and are antithetical in meaning.[1]

Infinitive Construct: 1 Kings 4:34 (5:14) - "And they came from all the people to hear the wisdom of Solomon.

Infinitive Absolute: Isaiah 3:16 - "The daughters of Zion . . . walk . . . walking and mincing."

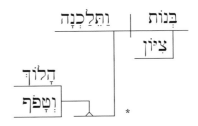

1. Thomas 0. Lambdin, *Introduction to Biblical Hebrew* (New York: Charles Scribner's Sons, 1971), pp. 129, 158-59.

CHAPTER II

Basic Illustrative Sermonic Organization

Every interpreter is encouraged to derive his outline for preaching directly from the diagrammed text. This is true for both verse by verse and topical messages. Therefore, the preacher will be preaching an outline that the Bible unfolds for him and not an outline placed or forced upon the Scripture. The following pattern for arriving at sermonic structure is intended to be a *guide* and *not* a *straitjacket.* Once the interpreter has mastered the general pattern, he then can incorporate some procedures meaningful to him which unfold the syntactical meaning of the biblical text. Whatever analysis the diagrammed text gives should be incorporated into the outline. If a word is there, do something with it in outline form so that it is understood in relation to the preaching of the major structure. In other words, for an outline of any Scripture text or passage of any length, all words in the diagrammatical analysis should appear in a workable outline based upon the diagram. This does not mean that the preacher must preach minor structure, but only that he understands its contribution and relationship to aid the communication of the main points and the major sub points. When expressions like "Jesus said," "thus saith the Lord," or addresses such as "my brethren" stand at the beginning of a diagrammed text or passage, and/or are repeated throughout the diagrammatical analysis, these do not always need to be outlined. If such supporting premises are not used in the body of the basic outline, then something must be done with them, and the only logical place is to incorporate as background or foundational material within the introduction to the message.

It is important that the student observe:

1. The <u>horizontal base lines</u> which form the basis for major points, major sub points and all subsequent points.

2. The <u>vertical lines</u> which divide the subject and predicate, predicate and direct object; and the <u>slanted lines</u> which indicate either

indirect object, predicate nominative or predicate adjective, subjective complement or objective complement. These vertical lines and slanted lines indicate <u>outline divisions</u> upon the horizontal base line.

3. The <u>modifiers</u> underneath the basic sentence unit(s) upon the horizontal base line change and enhance the meaning of the basic unit(s) immediately above.

4. <u>Transitional words</u> found between the horizontal base lines and connected by broken lines are not to be incorporated in the outline. These words help the preacher to form his transitional sentence or thoughts between points.

5. As nearly as possible the interpreter should watch the <u>parallel structure</u> his diagram gives to him. This is true, whether the parallel structure is horizontal or vertical.

6. Structure must <u>always have more than one point,</u> no matter whether it is a major point, major sub point or minor point.

7. Always think in terms of units. Proceed from the larger to the smaller. Observe horizontal and vertical units.

8. The wording of the major points of the outline <u>must develop</u> the proposition as stated and in parallel form.

9. Lay out the diagram neatly so that one has enough room for exegetical comments regarding each sentence unit and word in the diagram. Different colors of ink can be employed for the horizontal and vertical lines, the words of the text and the exegetical notes. Research well done is research accomplished for future ministry.

10. Verbs may be broken down into substructure showing the individual contribution of voice, tense, mood and etymology to the understanding of the whole. Likewise, other parts of speech may be outlined as to case, etymology or whatever analysis is evident within the usage of the word.

11. <u>Variations in sermon structure</u> will occur regarding the horizontal base lines (when there are 3 or more points, whether major, sub or, minor) depending how the exegete interprets his diagrammatical analysis.

12. Greek structure and Hebrew structure employ the same methodology, only reversed.

13. Detailed structure is suggested for the understanding of the biblical text. It is <u>not recommended</u> that the preacher preach minor structure to any audience. Major structure and major substructure are sufficient or the preacher will lose his congregation with detail. However, the preacher must understand the minor structure if he is going to accurately convey his major points. At the same time, it is recognized that certain texts may require some explanation of minor structure. Do not weary people with detailed outlines. Concentration on minor structure is for the preacher's benefit in preparation so he can convey the content precisely summarized to his people.

The essential pattern for sermonic organization based upon the diagrammatical analysis follows with observable variations. These examples are primary, not exhaustive.

Simple Sentence with Modifiers on Single Base Line

(Greek)

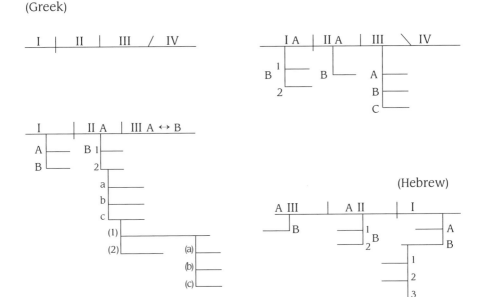

(Hebrew)

Compound Subjects, Verbs, Objects and Modifiers on Single Base Line

(Greek)

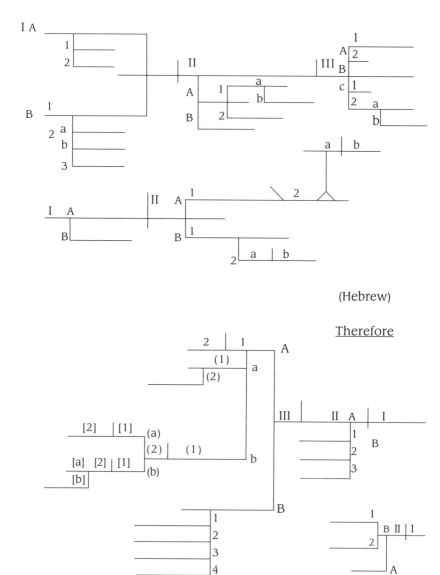

(Hebrew)

<u>Therefore</u>

Compound and Complex Sentences with Two or More Base Lines

(Greek)

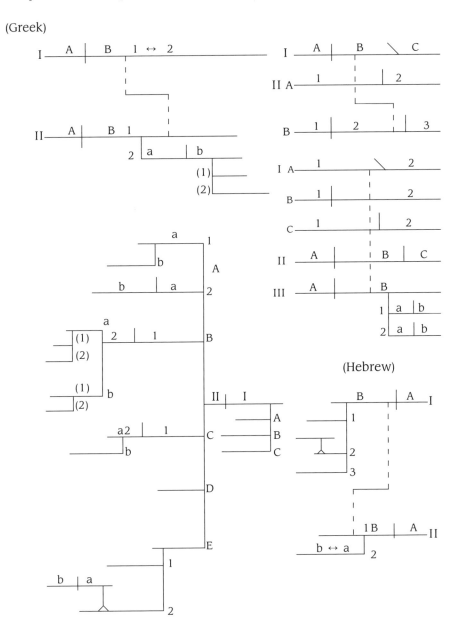

(Hebrew)

Sentences With Phrases and Clauses

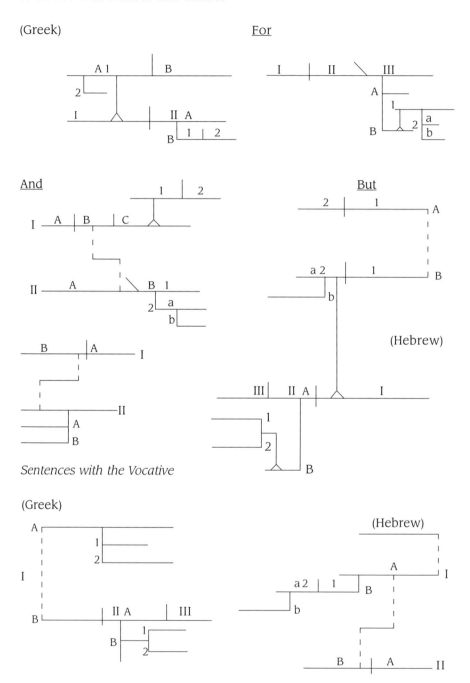

Sentences with the Vocative

Sentence Variations in Either Testament with a Simple Introductory Subject and Verb such as "Jesus said" or "The Lord of Hosts declared unto . . ."

(Greek)

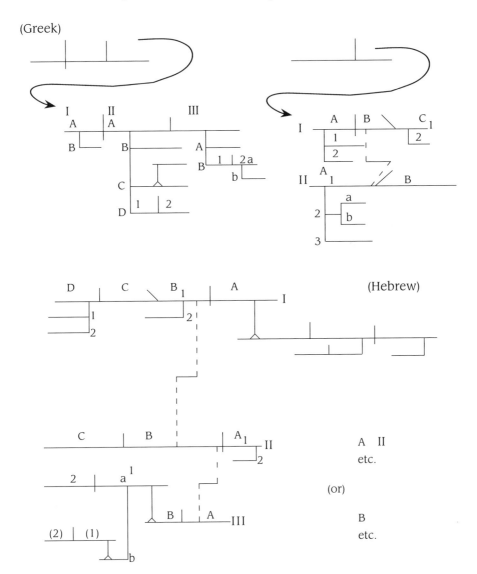

(Hebrew)

A   II
etc.

(or)

B
etc.

Sentences with Consistent Hebrew Parallelism on the Base Lines

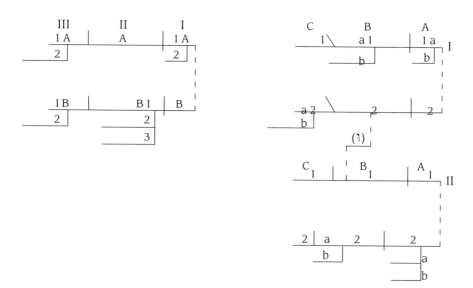

*Sentences with One Base Line and Many Modifiers under the Verb (only).
The Two Parallel Lines (═══) Indicate a Structural Break Homiletically
While Still Maintaining the Syntactical Relationship Grammatically.*

(Greek)

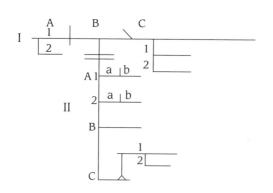

Hebrew structure is the
same, only reversed.

(Greek)

οὖν

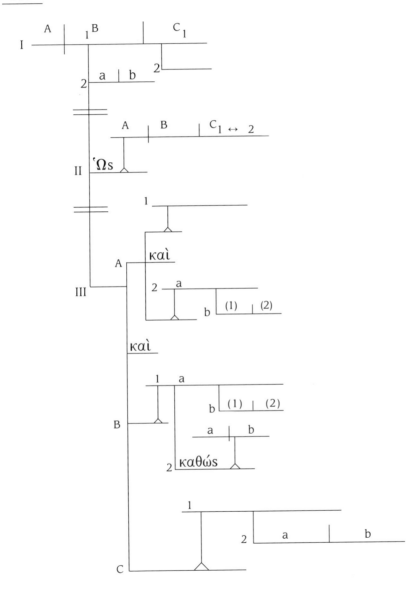

Sentences Having a Compound Unit with One Modifier

(Greek)

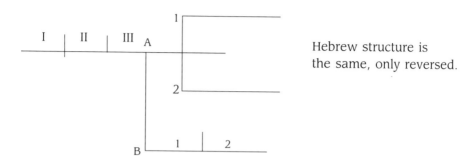

Hebrew structure is
the same, only reversed.

Sentences in Either Testament Which Have an Abundance of Words Horizontally. Use an "S" Hook When There is Not Enough Room on the Page.

(Hebrew)

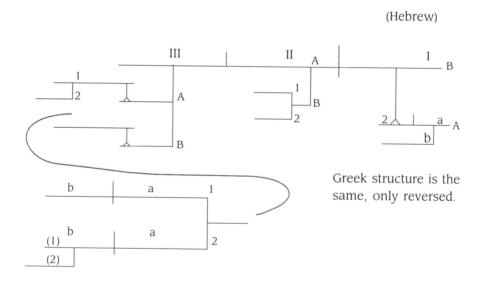

Greek structure is the
same, only reversed.

Contextual Analysis of Psalm 119:17-18

In regard to Psalm 119, Kidner writes, "This giant among the Psalms shows the full flowering of that 'delight . . . in the law of the Lord' which is described in Psalm 1, and gives its personal witness to the many-sided qualities of Scripture praised in Psalm 19:7ff." This Psalm is not only great in length, it is also great in personal impact upon the attentive reader.

The form of Psalm 119 involves an acrostic poem with each verse of each strophe beginning with the same Hebrew letter. Thus, it is a great literary work as well as a spiritual gold mine. Each stanza of the Psalm develops a particular unified thought.

The date and authorship of the Psalm are unknown. Perhaps it is best to see the Psalm as written around the time of the exile. Many suggest Daniel as the author, and the internal evidence of the Psalm fits this suggestion quite well.

The theme of Psalm 119 might be summarized as "applied bibliology." Using at least eight synonyms for the Word of God, the Psalm presents the Scriptures in a broad spectrum of the many-facetted gem that is God's written revelation. The young psalmist loved the Word and he presents its effect upon the believer's life in almost every conceivable aspect. There is a stress upon the theme of dependence upon God and His Word throughout the Psalm. The psalmist realizes deeply his need for God's enablement to understand the Word, and to be mastered by the Word.

Verses 17–18 begin the gimel (ג) stanza of the poem. The burden of this stanza deals with the sufficiency of God and His Word in times of difficulty. Out of obviously difficult circumstances, the young man of Psalm 119 cries out for enablement to meet severe pressures through the Word of God and dependence upon the God of the Word.

Diagrammatical Analysis and Sermonic Structure
of Psalm 119:17–18

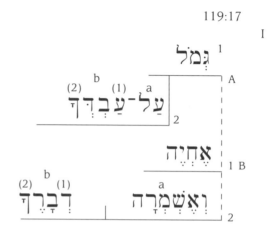

119:17

119:18

Analytical Outline of Psalm 119:17–18

Proposition—*Two requests* for divine enablement that the Psalmist finds necessary to be a man of God.

I. The request for enablement to *practice* the Word (119:17)

    A. The *statement* of the request for enablement to practice the Word (17a)

        1. The *essence* of the statement - גְּמֹל

          a. A simple plea (Qal imperative)

          b. A desire for favor (גְּמֹל)

        2. The *direction* of the statement - עַל־עַבְדְּךָ

          a. The direction *indicated* - עַל

          b. The direction *specified* - עַבְדְּךָ

            (1) Specified as to *person* - עֶבֶד

            (2) Specified as to *owner* - ךָ . . .

    B. The *outcome* of the request for enablement to practice the Word (17b)

        1. The *necessary accompaniment* to the outcome - אֶחְיֶה

          a. The *subject* of the accompaniment - א

          b. The *nature* of the accompaniment - חָיָה

          c. The *continuance* of the accompaniment - (imperfect tense)

        2. The *essence* of the outcome - וְאֶשְׁמְרָה דְבָרֶךָ

        (*Note:* The waw at the beginning of this phrase is a waw conjunctive, showing that there is a parallel connection between אֶחְיֶה and אֶשְׁמְרָה.)

          a. The *activity* of the essence of the outcome - וְאֶשְׁמְרָה

            (1) Involving active *obedience* - שָׁמַר

            (2) Involving active *determination* - (Qal cohortative)

          b. The *subject matter* of the essence of the outcome - דְבָרֶךָ

            (1) *Statement* of subject matter - דָּבָר (general term for God's Word)

            (2) *Author* of subject matter - ךָ . . .

II. The request for enablement to *understand* the Word (119:18)

    A. The *statement* of the request for enablement to understand the Word (18a)

        1. The *summary* of the statement - גַּל

            a. Involving a *plea* (imperative)

            b. Involving an *unveiling* - גָּלָה

            c. Involving *emphasis* - (Piel)

        2. The *area affected* in the statement - עֵינַי

            a. Being a figure of "understanding" - עַיִן

            b. Being a personal matter - (1 c.s. suffix)

    B. The *outcome* of the request for enablement to understand the Word (18b)

    (Note: The waw introducing this statement, being a waw conjunctive, could probably best be taken as "then.")

        1. The *specification* of the outcome - וְאַבִּיטָה

            a. Involving declarative *observation* - נָבַט

            b. Involving declarative *determination* (Hiphil cohortative)

        2. The *subject matter* of the outcome

            a. The *specifics* of the subject matter - נִכְלָאוֹת

            b. The *source* of the subject matter - מִתּוֹרָתֶךָ

                (1) The *direction* of the source - מִן

                (2) The *description* of the source - תּוֹרָה

                (3) The *author* of the source - ךָ . . .

Note: This analytical outline places the Hebrew word(s) to the right of each point. The following analytical outlines place the Greek word(s) to the right of each point. However, unless one is proficient in the original biblical languages, the English translation should definitely be used in place of the original word of the biblical text. The purpose for including the words of the text is so the exegete and/or interpreter knows exactly what part of the biblical text the workable sermonic outline is describing.

Contextual Analysis of 2 Peter 1:19-21

The Petrine authorship of II Peter is questioned by some Bible students. However, the question is really settled by; (1) the fact that the epistle itself states Petrine authorship (1:1; 3:1), and (2) by the testimony of the author that he saw the transfiguration personally (1:15–18).

The theme of II Peter involves "Christian growth through knowledge." The key word is "knowledge," which is repeated several times. The key verse is 3:18, "But *grow* in grace, and in the knowledge of our Lord and Savior, Jesus Christ." There are also the subthemes of the Second Coming (1:16 and 3:4–14) and of warning against false teachers (2:1–3:3).

As to the immediate context of 1:19–21, we find it set at the very end of chapter one. This chapter begins with the typical epistolary introduction in 1:1–2. The author then introduces the theme of the book in 1:3–11 by mentioning God's provision for spiritual birth and growth (1:3–4), and the believer's response in gratitude to it (1:5–11). From this point, the author proceeds to the authority for his epistle. This involves his pastoral concern and oversight (1:12–15), and God's confirmation of his message at the transfiguration (1:16–18). The authority of Scripture is then appealed to as the "more sure" foundation for the author's authority in 1:19–21. This text reveals (1) insight concerning the priority of the Word and (2) what the believer's practice in relation to the Word should be.

Diagrammatical Analysis and Sermonic Structure
of 2 Peter 1:19–21

1:19

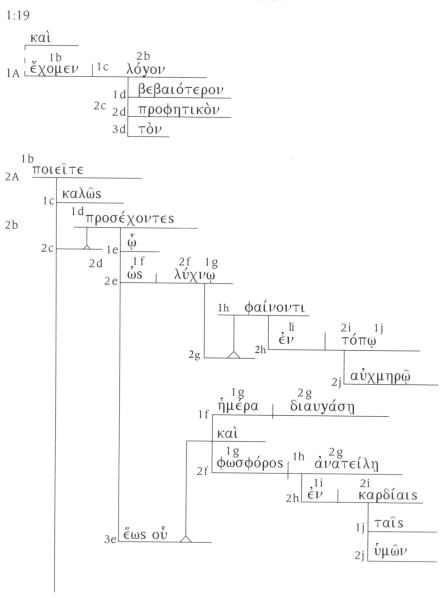

Note: Please observe an alternative method of outlining on this example than what is used throughout this manual. This method, 1A, 2A, 1b, 2b, etc. is more practical with detailed analysis, but it can be used with all diagrammed texts, long or short.

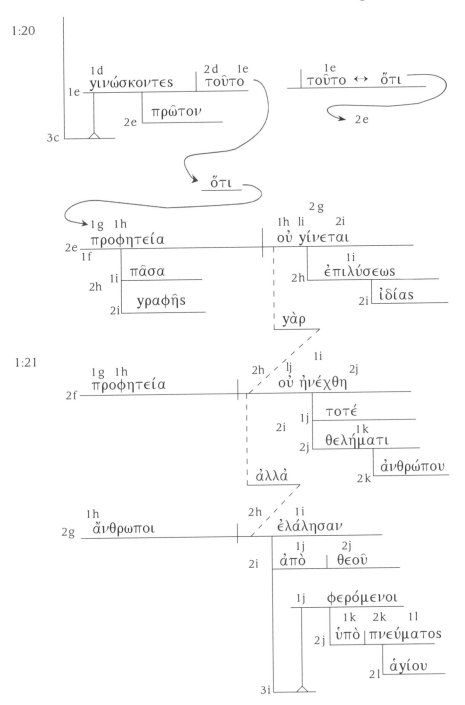

Analytical Outline of 2 Peter 1:19-21

Proposition—The apostle Peter makes two declarations concerning the place of God's Word in the lives of His people.

1A. The declaration concerning the *priority* of the Word (1:19a) ἔχομεν . . . λόγον - (Note: The καὶ introducing this clause relates it back to the previous context of the surety of the Lord's return. Here is one other evidence for this surety in addition to the parallel evidence of Peter as an eyewitness to the transfiguration in vs. 17–18.)

    1b. The possession of the priority item - ἔχομεν

        1c. It is continuous - (present tense)

        2c. It is personal - (first person plural)

        3c. It is ownership - ἔχω

    2b. The description of the priority item - βεβαιότερον . . . λόγον

        1c. The essence of the description - λόγον

        2c. The amplification of the description - βεβαιότερον . . . τον

            1d. Amplified as to trustworthiness - βεβαιότερον

                1e. Involving stability - βεβαίος

                2e. Involving comparison (comparative adjective)

            2d. Amplified as to character - προφητικὸν

            3d. Amplified as to individuality - τὸν

2A. The declaration concerning one's *practice* in relation to the Word (1:19b–21)

    1b. The practice summarized - ποιεῖτε

        1c. Summarized as continuous - present tense

        2c. Summarized as active - ποιέω

    2b. The practice spelled out - καλῶς . . . ἁγίου

        1c. Spelled out as to its quality - καλῶς

        2c. Spelled out as to its activity - προσέχοντες . . .

1d. The essence of the activity - προσέχοντες

  1e. It is constant - present tense

  2e. It is potential - conditional participle

  3e. It is attention - προσέχω

2d. The explanation of the activity - ᾧ . . .

  1e. Explained as to content - ᾧ

    1f. Involving reference - dative

    2f. Involving the Word - antecedent is λόγον

  2e. Explained by comparison - ὡς . . . αὐχμηρῷ

    1f. The comparison indicated - ὡς

    2f. The comparison specified - λύχνῳ . . . αὐχμηρῷ

      1g. As to its essence - λύχνῳ

      2g. As to its description - φαίνοντι . . .

        1h. Description of its activity - φαίνοντι

        2h. Description of its sphere- ἐν . . .

          1i. The sphere's boundary - ἐν

          2i. The sphere's designation - τόπῳ . . .

            1j. The title designated - τόπῳ

            2j. The quality designated - αὐχμηρῷ

  3e. Explained as to its continuance
(*Note*: ἕως οὗ which introduces this clause shows that it indicates duration. It answers the question, "how long should one take heed?")

    1f. Continuance until the Second Coming - ἡμέρα . . .

      1g. The eschatological designation of the Second Coming - ἡμέρα

      2g. The eschatological arrival of the Second Coming - διαυγάσῃ

        1h. It is an event - aorist

        2h. It is always potential - subjunctive

        3h. It is a dawning - διαυγάζω

    2f. Continuance until the personal result of the Second Coming - (*Note*: The kai; introducing this phrase sets it parallel to ἡμέρα διαυγάσῃ, as it is in fact a more personal description of the same event as to its impact on the individual believer experiencing it.)

1g. The metaphorical conveyor of the personal result - φωσφόρος

2g. The metaphorical arrival of the personal result - ἀνατείλῃ . . . ὑμῶν

    1h. The designation of the arrival - ἀνατείλῃ

        1i. It is an event - aorist

        2i. It is always potential - subjunctive

        3i. It is a rising - ἀνατέλλω

    2h. The sphere of the arrival - ἐν . . .

        1i. The boundaries of the sphere - ἐν

        2i. The area of the sphere - καρδίαις . . .

            1j. As to its realm - καρδίαις

            2j. As to its specification - ταῖς ὑμῶν

                1k. Specified by particularization - ταῖς

                2k. Specified by ownership - ὑμῶν

3c. Spelled out as to its attitude (20–21)

    1d. The explanation of the attitude - γινώσκοντες . . . ἁγίου

        1e. The explanation by means of summary - γινώσκοντες

           1f. It is constant - present tense

           2f. It is potential - conditional participle

           3f. It is experiential knowledge - γινώσκω

        2e. The explanation by means of emphasis - πρῶτον

    2d. The object affected by the attitude - τοῦτο . . . ἁγίου

        1e. The all-inclusive term for the object - τοῦτο

        2e. The explanation of the object - προφητεία . . .

           1f. The explanation itself involves the matter of interpretation - (*Note:* The recitative ὅτι introducing this clause indicates it is in effect serving as an appositional expansion of τοῦτο.) *See note at the end of this outline.*

                1g. The item for interpretation - προφητεία . . .

                    1h. The title of the item - προφητεία

2h. The amplification of the item - πᾶσα . . .

    1i. Its inclusiveness - πᾶσα

    2i. Its description - γραφῆς

2g. The improper approach to interpretation - οὐ . . . ἰδίας

    1h. The existence of the improper approach - οὐ . . . γίνεται

        1i. Is actually negated - οὐ

        2i. Is a state of being - γίνεται

            1j. Interpretation which is continuous - present tense

            2j. Interpretation which has an origin - γίνομαι

    2h. The description of the improper approach - ἐπιλύσεως ἰδίας

        1i. It is an unloosing - ἐπιλύσεως

        2i. It is one's own - ἰδίας

2f. The basis for the explanation involves the matter of inspiration (21). (*Note:* The γὰρ introducing verse 21 indicates it is the basis or reason for the explanation itself just having been given in verse 20. The reason for the attitude in regard to interpretation is the fact of inspiration.)

    1g. The negative side of the matter of inspiration (21a) - προφητεία . . . ἀνθρώπου

        1h. The item under consideration in the negative side - προφητεία

        2h. The process of the negative side of inspiration - οὐ . . . ἀνθρώπου

            1i. The essence of the process - οὐ ἠνέχθη

                1j. Involving actual negation - οὐ

2j. Involving an actual event - ἠνέχθη

    1k. The event is past - aorist

    2k. The event is a production - φέρω

2i. The details of the process - τότε . . .

    1j. Detailed as to time - τότε

    2j. Detailed as to instrumentality - θελήματι . . .

        1k. The determining factor of the instrumentality - θελήματι

        2k. The owner of the instrumentality - ἀνθρώπου

2g. The positive side of the matter of inspiration (21b) (*Note*: The conjunction of strong contrast, ἀλλὰ, introduces this clause, which is the antithesis of vs. 21b.)

    1h. The performers of the positive side - ἄνθρωποι

    2h. The performance of the positive side - ἐλάλησαν . . . ἁγίου

        1i. The activity of the performance - ἐλάλησαν

            1j. Being a past event -aorist

            2j. Being communication - λαλέω

        2i. The source of the performance - ἀπὸ θεοῦ

            1j. The direction of the source - ἀπὸ

            2j. The Person of the Source - θεοῦ

        3i. The means of the performance - φερόμενοι . . . ἁγίου

            1j. The description of the means - φερόμενοι

                1k. It is constant - present tense (simultaneous with main verb)

2k. It is affected by an outside source - passive voice

3k. It is a carrying - φέρω

2j. The personal agency of the means - ὑπὸ . . .

1k. The indication of the personal agency - ὑπὸ

2k. The Person of the personal agency - πνεύματος ἁγίου

11. His title - πνεύματος

21. His character - ἁγίου

*Note: This thorough, detailed and in-depth outline structure into minor points is done to show the technical procedure which is the outline organization suggested by the passage itself. However, a *more effective sermonic outline* would be to make a *third major point* beginning with the appositional ὅτι clause (1:20-21). This means a rewording of the proposition and possibly the other two major points. Remember, the suggestion is *not* to preach minor structure in outline fashion but to understand its contribution to the explanation of the text and the major points.

Contextual Analysis of Mark 6:20

The impressions recorded in Mark 6:20 are given in the wider context of Jesus' Galilean ministry (1:14–9:50). In Mark 5:1–43 Jesus performs a series of miracles. Following these Jesus returns to Nazareth, His home town, where He is rejected (6:1–6). The immediate setting details the mission of the twelve and the excitement caused by the miracles wrought through their hands (6:7–13). Their ministry naturally spread abroad the name and fame of Jesus. This was good news to the mass of people in Galilee, but it was not good tidings to King Herod (6:14–16). When Herod heard of Jesus' mighty works, his superstitious nature figured that John the Baptist was risen from the dead while others saw Jesus as one of the prophets (6:15).

The steps in the lurid story of the death of John the Baptist are recorded in Mark 6:17–29. Herod had an incestuous union with Herodias, the wife of his brother Philip (17). John rebuked the monarch's sin and was consequently imprisoned (17–18). Later Herod had a feast prepared to honor his own birthday (21). The daughter of Herodias, Salome, disgraced herself in a dance before Herod who made a vow to give to her whatever she asked up to half of his kingdom (22–23). Salome inquired of her mother and demanded that John the Baptist be beheaded (24–25). Herod fulfilled his vow but he was deeply regretful that he allowed himself to be so pliable in the hands of his wicked Queen (26–28). John's disciples bury him (29) and the twelve report to Jesus what they had done and taught on their tour (30). Jesus, pleased with the report, but saddened about the death of His faithful forerunner, changes His pattern of ministry by leading the twelve on a series of four withdrawals from Galilee, returning there intermittently (6:31–9:50).

In the unfolding of the narrative (6:14–29), it is clear that the purpose of John's imprisonment was because Herodias wanted John put to death (6:17–19), which later he was (6:27). Herod obstinately refused to yield to his wife's request. The reason for such refusal is explained in Mark 6:20. Herod had observed in John a pattern of life different from his own. Herein emerge two qualities that commended John the Baptist as a preacher and servant of God before Herod. These same qualities should characterize all preachers at all times.

Analysis Word Sheets of Mark 6:20

WORD	Tense or Part of Speech	Voice	Mode or Case	Person	Gender	Number	Etymology	Contextual Meaning
ὁ	Article		Nom		M	S	ὁ	the

Discussion: Goes with Ἡρῴδης, indicating the person is known and designating Herod as a specific individual   BAG - p. 552

WORD								
γὰρ	Conj.						γὰρ	for

Discussion: Used to express cause, inference, continuation, or explanation of (from) preceding verses in context   BAG - p. 151

Ἡρῴδης	Proper Noun		Nom		M	S	Ἡρῴδης	Herod Antipas

Discussion: Son of Herod the Great mentioned in the New Testament for his clash with John the Baptist (among other things)   BAG - p. 347

ἐφοβεῖτο	Imperfect	M	Ind.	3	M	S	φοβέω	fear someone or something

Discussion: Herod feared John - an action going on in past time simultaneously with his action

τόν	Article		Acc		M	S	ὁ	the

Discussion: Goes with the known Ἰωάννην

Ἰωάννην	Proper Noun		Acc		M	S	Ἰωάννης	John

Discussion: John the Baptist the direct object of Herod's fear.

εἰδὼς	Perf. Ptcp.	A	Nom		M	S	οἶδα	knew

Discussion: Herod knew from the past, the continuing character of John the Baptist.

αὐτὸν	Pers. Pro.		Acc		M	S	αὐτός	him

Discussion: Emphasizes a subject already known

ἄνδρα	Noun		Acc		M	S	ἀνήρ	man

Discussion: Man in contrast to woman, used with adjectives to emphasize the dominant characteristic of a man   BAG - p. 61

δίκαιον	adj.		Acc		M	S	δίκαιος	upright, just

Discussion: John is described as a man who lived in accordance with the laws of God.

καὶ	Conj.						καὶ	and

Discussion: Continuative in describing the character of John and coordinating them

ἅγιον	adj.		Acc		M	S	ἅγιος	consecrated to God, holy

Discussion: John is described as a man whose character was a quality like that of God.

Analysis Word Sheets of Mark 6:20 *(continued)*

WORD	Tense or Part of Speech	Voice	Mode or Case	Person	Gender	Number	Etymology	Contextual Meaning
καί	Conj.						καί	and
Discussion: Continuative in coordinating the action of the imperfect verbs							
συνετήρει	Imperfect	M	Ind.	3	M	S	συντηρέω	protect, defend
Discussion: Herod kept and guarded John from harm and ruin of a plot.							
αὐτόν	Pers.Pro.		Acc		M	S	αὐτός	him
Discussion: John the Baptist was the object continually of Herod's protection.							
καί	Conj.						καί	and
Discussion: Continuative in coordinating the action of the imperfect verbs							
ἀκούσας	Aor. ptcp.	A	Nom		M	S	ἀκούω	to hear, listen
Discussion: Herod heard John speak and the action is observed in its entirety. (constative)							
αὐτοῦ	Pers. Pro.		Gen.		M	S	αὐτός	him
Discussion: The sense verb ἀκούω takes the gen. to emphasize the known person Herod heard.							
πολλά	Adj. used as a subst.		(noun) Acc		N	pl	πολύς	much or many, greatly
Discussion: Acc. use as an adverb to show the degree of the verbal intensity							
ἐποίει	Imperfect	A	Ind.	3	M	S	ποιέω (ἀπορέω) (ἠπόρει)	disturbed Thayer - 66 BAG - 97
Discussion: Herod was in perplexity about many things or much perplexed. (Thayer - 66)							
καί	Conj.						καί	and
Discussion: Continuative in coordinating the action of the imperfect verbs.							
ἡδέως	adv.						ἡδέως	gladly, with pleasure
Discussion: Indicates how Herod heard John.							
αὐτοῦ	Pers. Pro.		Gen.		M	S	αὐτός	him
Discussion: The sense verb ἀκούω takes the gen. to emphasize the known person Herod heard.							
ἤκουεν	Imperfect	A	Ind.	3	M	S	ἀκούω	to hear
Discussion: Describes the continuous action as going on at some time in the past.							

Diagrammatical Analysis and Sermonic Structure
of Mark 6:20

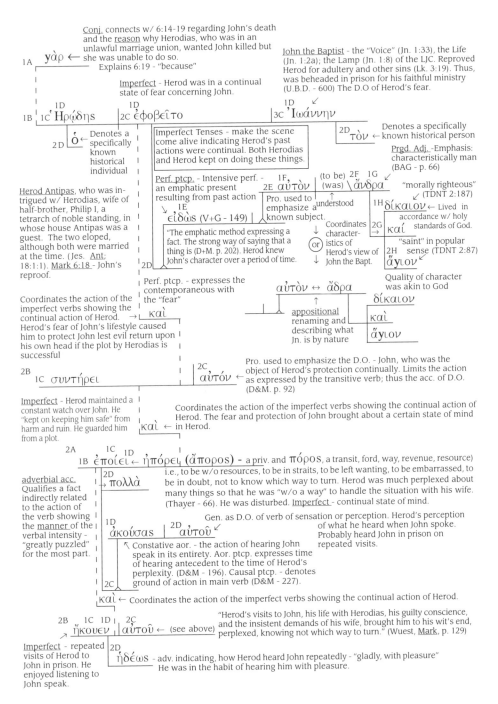

ANALYTICAL OUTLINE OF MARK 6:20

Proposition—Two parts regarding Herod's view of the essential greatness of John the Baptist

1A. Herod's Testimony to the Essential Greatness of John the Baptist - 6:20a
  1B. The Statement of the Testimony
    1C. The Possessor of the Statement
      ID. The Possessor Identified - Ἡρῴδης
      2D. The Possessor Particularized - ὁ
    2C. The Action of the Statement
      1D. The essence of the action - ἐφοβεῖτο
        1E. It is continual - Imperfect
        2E. It is personal - 3 ms
        3E. It is indirect - Middle voice
        4E. It is factual - Ind. Mood
        5E. It is defined - root "to be seized with fear"
      2D. The expression of the action
        1E. It is emphasized - εἰδὼς
          1F. As intensive - perfect
          2F. As contemporaneous - ptcp.
          3F. As existing - active voice
          4F. As designated - Nom. case
          5F. As personal - M.S.
          6F. As defined - knowledge known
        2E. It is described
          1F. As a known subject - αὐτὸν
          2F. As a distinct person
            1G. In contrast to woman - ἄνδρα
            2G. In comparison to character
              1H. Character of living - δίκαιον
              2H. Character of godliness - ἅγιον

3C. The Object of the Statement

  1D. The object identified - Ἰωάννην

  2D. The object particularized - τὸν

2B. The Continuation of the Testimony

  1C. The Action of the Continuation - συντήρει

    1D. It is continual - Imperfect

    2D. It is produced - active voice

    3D. It is factual - ind. mood

    4D. It is personal - 3 ms.

    5D. It is defined - preservation

  2C. The Object of the Continuation - αὐτόν

2A. Herod's Recognition of the Essential Greatness of John the Baptist - 6:20b

  1B. The Involvement of the Recognition

    1C. The Affect of the Involvement

      1D. The intensity of the affect - ἐποίει

        1E. It is continual - imperfect

        2E. It is produced - active voice

        3E. It is factual - ind. mood

        4E. It is personal - 3 ms

        5E. It is defined - disturbed

      2D. The manner of the affect - πολλὰ

    2C. The Expression of the Involvement

      1D. The action of the expression - ἀκούσας

        1E. Viewed in its entirety - constative aorist

        2E. Viewed by its cause - causal ptcp.

        3E. Viewed in its production - active voice

        4E. Viewed by its designation - nom. case

        5E. Viewed by its individuality - MS

        6E. Viewed by its definition - heard declarations

      2D. The object of the expression - αὐτοῦ

2B. The Enjoyment of the Recognition
   1C. The Action of the Enjoyment
      1D. The statement of the action - ἤκουεν
         1E. It is continual - imperfect
         2E. It is produced - active voice
         3E. It is factual - ind. mood
         4E. It is personal - 3 ms
         5E. It is defined - heard declarations
      2D. The degree of the action - ἡδέως
   2C. The Object of the Enjoyment - αὐτοῦ

Sermonic Outline of Mark 6:20

Proposition—Two Qualities that Commend John the Baptist as a Preacher

1A. *Quality of a Respected Character* - 6:20a
   1B. Based upon a Continual Observation - a man in touch with God
      1C. Observed by a person of authority - "Herod"
      2C. Observed through a condition of reverence - "feared . . . knowing . . ."
      3C. Observed in a servant of God - "John"
   2B. Resulted in a Constant Protection - "kept on keeping him safe"

Transition: A respected character is not a dead-end street. It is harmonized with attraction and allures others to oneself.

2A. *Quality of a Winsome Messenger* - 6:20b
   1B. Began by Exercising his Listener
      1C. With a development of intense puzzlement - "very perplexed"
      2C. Upon a sensation of attentive listening - "having heard him"
   2B. Developed into Captivating his Listener - "heard gladly with pleasure"

Index of Biblical References

Genesis
1:1   14, 16, 21, 24
1:2   20, 24
1:14   26
4:8   49
12:12   68
12:13   67, 68
13:16b   60
22:3   28
37:5   23, 46
37:6   37, 48
37:7   41
37:13   17
37:14   21
37:18   46
37:22   33
37:25   40
37:27   33
37:29   21
38:25   35
40:8   32
41:57   29, 30
42:2   38, 66
42:4   18
42:6   17
42:7   19, 20
42:9   42, 43
42:10   66
42:21   31
42:25   70
42:28   32
43:7   46
43:18   52
44:14   22
44:24   49
44:32b   58, 59
45:1a   39

Exodus
3:14   14

Deuteronomy
7:7   72
8:3   70
28:67   34

1 Samuel
10:16   46

1 Kings
4:34   75

Job
10:14   55, 56

Psalms
34:11   33
119:17–18   86, 87, 88

Isaiah
1:9   57
3:16   75

Hosea
14:1   64

Matthew
2:2   44
2:13   33
3:1   39
4:4   65
5:43   65
6:5   74
7:28   50
9:28   74
9:33   69
10:38   47
11:14   74
12:44   50, 51
14:32   69
15:1   22
16:13   45
24:14   62
28:15   35

Mark
6:20   99–103, 106
12:12   44
12:38   74

Luke
21:6   69

John
1:12   45
1:13   13
1:14   17, 22, 23, 62
1:17   22
1:19   32
1:20   13
1:28   13, 61
2:23   61
3:2   14
3:8   62
3:14   31
3:16   14, 19, 62
3:17   64
3:22   61
3:23   61
3:29   40
3:36   62
4:2   62
4:38b   26, 27
4:42   61
5:7   61
5:26   62
5:30   15
6:36   62
6:41   61
6:50   38
7:10   61
7:38   62
7:39   15
7:44   15
8:16   54
8:22   61
8:31   62
8:36   62
8:58   61
9:1   61
9:17   61
9:18   61
9:22   61
10:11   19, 20

John (continued)
10:38	52, 53
10:42	13
11:5	16, 23, 24
11:6	29, 30
11:8	16
11:27	67
11:32	56
11:35	14
12:1	48
12:2	16
13:9	62
13:35	62
14:3	61
14:17	63
14:19	52
14:26	70
15:4	61, 62
16:7	62
17:3	17
17:6	15
17:14	62
18:1	61
19:15	31
19:17	61
19:37	61
19:41	61
20:2	61
20:12	61
20:20	62
20:31	14

Acts
20:27	1

Romans
1:27	62
1:28	45

Romans (continued)
5:15	62
7:18	43
7:24	34
8:35	31
10:6	62
12:1	15

1 Corinthians
11:2	51
14:16	62
15:8	62

2 Corinthians
6:15	62
7:8	54
12:11	74

Galatians
3:1	63
5:18	55

Ephesians
1:1	20
1:4	71
5:1	32
5:28	74

Philippians
1:20	37
1:21	43
2:6	44
2:12	19
2:13	42
3:4	41
4:8	11
4:15	18
4:6	21

1 Thessalonians
5:19	32

1 Timothy
2:1	62

Titus
2:12	25

Hebrews
12:1	72
12:2	72
4:2	53

James
4:10	27

1 Peter
3:14	59, 60
5:8	18

2 Peter
1:19-21	90, 91, 93
3:3	68

1 John
1:8	58
2:5	62

3 John
8	36
12c	36

Jude
8	73
10	73

Bibliography

Adams, Frank P. *Diagrams and Analyses.* Indianapolis: Normal Publishing House, 1886.

Bohnett, Earl Marcus. "Principles and Methods of Biblical Research." Unpublished class syllabus. Baptist Bible College, Denver, Colorado, February 1966.

Bohrer, Dick. *Easy English.* Portland, Oregon; Multnomah Press, 1977.

Chamberlain, William Douglas. *An Exegetical Grammar of the Greek New Testament.* Grand Rapids: Baker Book House, 1941.

Crouch, Owen L. *Expository Preaching and Teaching - Hebrews.* Joplin, Missouri: College Press Publishing Company, 1983.

Dana, H.E., and Mantey, Julius R. *A Manual Grammar of the Greek New Testament.* New York: The Macmillan Company, 1927.

Davidson, A.B. *Hebrew Syntax.* Third Edition. Edinburgh: T. & T. Clark, 1974.

DeVincent-Hayes, Nan. *Grammer & Diagramming Sentences.* Eugene, Oregon: Garlic Press, 1995.

Ebner, Louise M. *Learning English with the Bible.* English Grammar Diagrams Based on the Book of Joshua. AMG Publishers, 1983.

Emery, Donald W. *Sentence Analysis.* New York: Holt, Rinehart and Winston, 1961.

Fink, Paul R. "A Design of the System and Facilities to be used in the Speech and Homiletics Program of Grace Theological Seminary, Winona Lake, Indiana." Unpublished paper. The University of Southern California, July 1970.

Grassmick, John D. *Principles and Practice of Greek Exegesis.* Second Edition. Dallas: Dallas Theological Seminary, 1974.

Greenberg, Moshe. *Introduction to Hebrew.* Englewood Cliffs, New Jersey: Prentice-Hall, Inc., 1965.

Hodges, John C. *Harbrace College Handbook.* New York: Harcourt, Brace and Company, 1951.

Lambdin, Thomas O. *Introduction to Biblical Hebrew.* New York: Charles Scribner's Sons, 1971.

Ludgin, Donald H. "Diagram of a Sentence." In *The World Book Encyclopedia.* Vol. 17, 1972.

Mickelsen, A. Berkeley. *Interpreting the Bible.* Grand Rapids: Wm. B. Eerdmans Publishing Company, 1963.

Pence, R. W., and Emery, D. W. *A Grammar of Present-Day English.* New York: The Macmillan Company, 1963.

Ramey, Robert F. "Diagramming of Grammar." Unpublished paper. Grace Theological Seminary, March 1971.

Reed, Alonzo and Kellogg, Brainerd. *Higher Lessons in English.* New York: Charles E. Merrill Company, 1909.

Smart, Walter Kay. *English Review Grammar.* New York: Appleton-Century-Crofts, Inc., 1940.

Taft, Kendall B., McDermott, John Francis, and Jensen, Dana O. *The Technique of Composition.* New York: Rinehart & Company, Inc., 1941.

Vaughan, Curtis and Gideon, Virtus E. *A Greek Grammar of the New Testament.* Nashville: Broadman Press, 1979.

Vivian, Charles and Jackson, Bernetta. *English Composition.* New York: Barnes & Noble, Inc., 1961.

Vos, Howard F. *Effective Bible Study.* Grand Rapids: Zondervan Publishing House, 1956.

Walsh, J. Martyn and Walsh, Anna Kathleen. *Plain English Handbook.* Cincinnati: McCormick-Mathers Publishing Company, Inc., 1966.

Watts, J. Wash. *A Survey of Syntax in the Hebrew Old Testament.* Grand Rapids: Wm. B. Eerdmans Publishing Company, 1964.

Webster, Noah. *Webster New Twentieth Century Dictionary of the English Language.* Cleveland: The World Publishing Company, 1971.

What Others are Saying:

The meaning of God's Word is dependent not only upon the words that are used, but also upon their syntactical relationship to one another. Grammatical analysis is the key to an accurate understanding of the Word of God.

One who would interpret the Scripture accurately and properly and who would have a truly biblical theology will find Dr. Kantenwein's book an indispensable tool for an accurate analysis and understanding of the Word of God. It will show step by step "how to do it." *Diagrammatical Analysis* is heartily recommended.

> — *Paul R. Fink, Th.D., Professor of Religion, Liberty University*

As the man of God declares the whole counsel of God, he must handle accurately that precious Word of Truth. His methodology of preparation should be in harmony with the biblical doctrine of inspiration.

Consequently, the syntax of any passage that he wishes to expound must be organizationally determinative. In other words, the organization needs to come from the text rather than being imposed upon the text.

Diagrammatical Analysis by Dr. Lee Kantenwein provides valuable assistance toward this end. Beginning with pictures of syntax (i.e. the diagrams) he illustrates how to put muscles and flesh upon these important skeletons. Once this strategic methodology is adopted and adapted, the apologetical impact of the resultant messages is unshackled since the Spirit will be attending what He originally conveyed.

> — *George J. Zemek, Jr., Th.D., Director of Ministry Training Center,*
> *The Bible Church, Little Rock, Arkansas*